INSIDE SECRETS TO CROWDFUND INVESTING

Follow Jane's Journey:
See How a New Generation
Builds Wealth with
Purpose, Passion, and Profit

By
Karen Rands

Designed, and Edited by Paramount Ghost Writers
Published by KYR Media

ISBN: 978-0-9991815-1-5
BUSINESS & ECONOMICS / Personal Finance / Investing
BUSINESS & ECONOMICS / Investment & Securities / Venture Capital
BUSINESS & ECONOMICS / Personal Finance / Wealth Management

Compassionalist and Compassionate Capitalist are trademarks and the Kugarand Theory of Private Equity; the Wealth & Liquidity Calculator, the Angel Profitability Blueprint are copyrighted content of Kugarand Capital Holdings, LLC.

Investment Disclaimer

The information contained in this book is provided for informational and entertainment purposes only and is not intended as investment, legal, tax, or financial advice.

Investing in startups and the equity of private companies at any stage is inherently risky and involves the potential for total loss of capital. Investing through crowdfunding platforms is no less risky. Private equity investments are typically illiquid, speculative, and not suitable for all investors. You should never invest more than you can afford to lose.

Always perform your own due diligence. Seek the counsel of financial and legal advisors, accountants, and industry professionals with direct experience in private equity investing. Consider your own risk tolerance before making any investment decisions.

The author and publisher disclaim any liability for investment outcomes related to the material presented in this book or on affiliated websites.

Dedication

This book is dedicated to the generation of women and people of color who were unable to catch the train to wealthy land because of the laws and regulations that restricted their access to capital to start a business, borrow money for a business, or even buy a home.

This book is dedicated to the up-and-coming generations of strivers who feel they can never catch up because they are priced out of real estate investments, and the turmoil of the stock and crypto markets makes it seem they can never get in on 'the ground floor'.

This book is for all those who desire to create wealth with impact and want to join a *community* of Compassionate Capitalists who understand problems can be solved and wealth can be shared as innovative startups and hard-working local businesses poised for growth get the capital they need to succeed. You can ride their wave of success and prosperity.

Forward

By Devin D. Thorpe

Author of How to Make Money with Impact Crowdfunding, CEO and Founder of SuperCrowd, Inc

For more than a decade, I have been writing about and championing the power of using our money to make the world a better place. I've seen firsthand how a single investment, no matter how small, can ripple outward to support a family, revitalize a community, or fuel an innovation that solves a problem we all care about. The most exciting part of this journey has been witnessing a fundamental shift in the world of finance; a shift from an exclusive, closed-door club to an open, accessible movement for everyone.

This is the world of crowdfunding, and it is a world where you belong; you are an investor. Whether you own a home, contribute to a 401(k), or have simply saved up for a rainy day, you are already making financial decisions that shape your future. The question is no longer about whether you are an investor but what kind of investor you want to be.

That is why Karen Rands' book, Inside Secrets to Crowdfund Investing, is so essential for this moment. Karen is a trailblazer who has spent decades in the trenches, guiding entrepreneurs to funding and empowering investors to build wealth with meaning. In these pages, she doesn't just talk about investing; she invites you on a journey. She has poured her immense knowledge and passion into creating a roadmap for a new generation of what she masterfully calls "Compassionalists," investors who lead with purpose, passion, and, yes, a healthy focus on profit.

The ideas in this book resonate deeply with the principles I share in my own work. Karen and I are aligned in our core belief that the 2012 JOBS Act was more than just legislation; it was a declaration of economic democracy. It tore down the velvet ropes that for nearly a century kept everyday people from participating in one of the most powerful wealth-creation engines: backing private companies on the ground floor.

In How to Make Money with Impact Crowdfunding, I argue that focusing on making a profit is critical because when you make money, you can reinvest it to amplify your impact infinitely. Karen's work powerfully reinforces this idea. She understands that compassion and capitalism are not opposing forces; they are two sides of the same powerful coin. When you invest in a profitable business that is solving a real-world problem, you create a sustainable cycle of good. A successful company can continue its mission, create jobs, and deliver returns that allow you to support the next great entrepreneur.

What I admire most about this book is its profound accessibility. The world of private equity can be intimidating, filled with complex jargon and abstract concepts. Karen brilliantly cuts through the noise by introducing us to "Jane," a character whose story makes the entire process feel tangible, relatable, and, most importantly, achievable. Following Jane's journey from a curious novice to a confident investor provides a practical, step-by-step illustration of how to:

• Assess your own financial landscape to invest safely and strategically.

• Build a diversified portfolio that balances risk with reward, using frameworks like her "Angel Profitability Blueprint".

● Perform the due diligence necessary to separate promising opportunities from hopeful fantasies.

● Invest in what you know and love, turning your unique life experience into an investor's edge.

This last point is a secret weapon that cannot be overstated. You don't need a fancy degree or a Wall Street background to be a successful investor. Your experience as a parent, a nurse, a teacher, or a tech enthusiast gives you insights that professionals may lack. Karen empowers you to trust that knowledge and use it to find and vet companies that align with your expertise and your values.

The SuperCrowd is growing every day—a movement of millions of ordinary people who are realizing they have the power to fund the future they want to see. We are backing diverse founders such as women, people of color, and others who have been systematically overlooked by traditional finance at rates that put the venture capital world to shame. We are investing in our local communities, supporting the small businesses that make our neighborhoods vibrant places to live.

Inside Secrets to Crowdfund Investing is more than a book; it is a key that unlocks the door to this movement. It provides the education, the tools, and the encouragement you need to step through with confidence. Read it carefully. Absorb the lessons from Jane's journey. Use the frameworks Karen provides to build your own strategy.

The financial world is changing for the better, becoming more inclusive, more impactful, and more human. You have a role to play in that transformation. Welcome to the SuperCrowd. Let's get to work.

About the Author

Karen Rands is a trailblazer in the world of early-stage investing, dedicated to making wealth-building strategies accessible to those historically excluded from them. Having worked with startups to get funding, first at IBM as a Complex Opportunity Business Manager and later as the Managing Director for The Network of Business Angels and Investors in Atlanta, Karen has gained first-hand knowledge of the motivations and best practices of successful angel investors. She first turned this into the financial literacy primer for sophisticated investors with her book *Inside Secrets to Angel Investing: Step-by-Step Strategies to Leverage Private Equity Investment for Passive Wealth Creation.* With countless interviews and speaking engagements, Karen is considered a thought leader in investor education and understands the motivations of angel investors and venture capitalists. She has spent decades helping individuals discover how to invest in entrepreneurs and innovative businesses, long before they go public or get acquired.

Karen is the founder of the Compassionate Capitalist™ Movement, a mission-driven initiative to democratize access to early-stage investing. She has enlightened thousands through her top-ranked podcast, *The Compassionate Capitalist™ Show*, her best-selling book (*Inside Secrets*), and her digital training platform, *The Compassionalist™ Academy*.

Through her work, Karen has challenged outdated paradigms of wealth creation. She understands that many people were left behind by laws that, until recently, restricted access to investment opportunities, particularly for women, people of color, and those outside traditional wealth circles. Her latest book is a direct response to this systemic exclusion, designed to help a new generation of investors leap the wealth gap and build financial independence by investing in the innovation economy.

With a background in venture consulting, capital formation, and investor relations, Karen continues to empower everyday individuals to become Compassionate Capitalists—investing not just for profit but for impact.

Preface

For generations, wealth creation in America has been limited to a privileged few. Laws and regulations, whether intentional or not, have historically restricted access to the very investment opportunities that create long-term financial independence. Real estate has long been the gateway to wealth, dating back to the era of homesteading and the economic stimulus of the GI Bill that launched the middle class. Yet Real Estate ownership was challenging and inaccessible to many—especially women and people of color—until just a generation ago. Meanwhile, early-stage private equity investing, one of the most lucrative asset classes, was off-limits to all but millionaires until the 2012 JOBS Act changed the game.

The result? Entire communities have been left out of wealth-building for decades. Even today, with access to public stocks and crypto, many people still feel shut out. Stocks are volatile, crypto is unpredictable, and real estate investing has become so expensive that younger generations, especially millennials, find it nearly impossible to use it as a pathway to wealth.

But what if there was another way?

That's why I wrote this book. I want to inspire and equip those who feel left behind, whether by outdated laws, financial barriers, or simply a lack of access to education about their options. Investing in entrepreneurs through equity crowdfunding and angel investing offers an alternative path to building wealth, one that is more purpose-driven, more profitable, and more accessible than traditional investing.

This book is not just about making money—it's about shifting the paradigm of wealth creation. It's about turning everyday people into investors who fuel innovation, job creation, and economic growth. It's about bringing 500,000 new investors into the market, bridging the wealth gap, and proving that impact-driven investing is the future of capitalism.

My aha moment came when I was preparing for my dad's passing, reviewing his collection of mementos and files, and learning anew his own impact as an inventor and entrepreneur. I was well aware that there were not enough investors to invest in all the worthy companies. I had seen it month after month at the angel investor events I organized. Inspired by my own father's journey to take risks and strive to solve problems he saw as opportunities, I said to myself:

'No one talks about it; are they not aware or not concerned that there isn't enough capital for startups and growing businesses?

Why is angel investing, investing in entrepreneurs and sharing in their success as they strive and build their business, such a secret?

What if we could unlock the capital on the sidelines, in people's banking and savings accounts, and partner it with appropriate debt capital and expand the available pool of capital?

Our economy would have never-ending growth if qualified businesses could get the funding they needed, products and services solved problems, and more jobs were created.

How do I shift that paradigm and bring more investors to the market to discover the 2nd greatest way to create wealth??

How could "I" do this when there isn't a movement behind it?

And then it occurred to me… <u>if not me, then who?</u>

What is my road map to make this happen?

✔ *Start the Compassionate Capitalist Movement— shifting the conversation around wealth creation to include investing in entrepreneurs as a viable, high-return asset class.*

✔ *Educate and empower new investors with books, digital courses, and direct mentorship.*

✔ *Speak on the economic power of community-driven investment to create generational wealth.*

✔ *Host a globally ranked business podcast amplifying the message of Compassionate Capitalism; wealth-creating for Founders and Investors.*

✔ Launch the Compassionate Capitalist (Compassionalist) Academy, a platform for training curious and committed investors in equity crowdfunding and angel investing.

This book is your invitation to be part of the movement. If you've ever felt like wealth creation was reserved for someone else, this is your chance to change that. It's time to take control, invest with impact, and become a Compassionate Capitalist.

Let's get started.

Contents

Introduction: The Making of a "Compassionalist"

For generations, investing in high-growth businesses was a privilege reserved for the wealthy; the dream of seeing your money grow as start-ups expanded, creating jobs, and transforming industries felt out of reach for most people. The idea of becoming part of something big, investing in companies that could change the world, was typically only available to those with deep pockets, large portfolios, and exclusive connections.

However, everything changed in 2012 with the passage of the Jumpstart Our Business Start-ups Act, popularly known as the JOBS Act, which legalized equity crowdfunding; suddenly, anyone could invest in start-ups and early-stage companies, regardless of their financial status. The JOBS Act created a legal shift and a cultural transformation that opened up new doors for regular, working-class people to participate in the kind of investing that was once solely in the hands of the wealthy.

Crowdfunding and Angel Investing remain largely unknown to many because these investment opportunities were kept under wraps for a long time. Unlike stocks, the lack of word-of-mouth and public discourse has not encouraged individuals to explore these options. Most "Main Street" investors remain unaware that they can invest in entrepreneurs as they launch and grow their businesses and share in their success.

Other than reality TV shows like *Shark Tank* and *Lion's Den,* there are no characters or storylines in prominent television shows talking about the latest crowdfunding or angel investing trends. And although there aren't celebrities or famous athletes appearing in commercials *promoting investing in entrepreneurs,* as they do with stocks or cryptocurrencies, occasionally you'll see announcements that celebrities like Ashton Kutcher, Vanessa Williams, and Jay-Z are investing in startups and small businesses.

Perhaps the closest we have to an example of actions speak louder than words as a 'celebrity endorsement' of crowdfunding investing would be *"Mr. Wonderful"* Kevin O'Leary's purchase of equity ownership in StartEngine Crowdfunding. StartEngine was an up-and-coming equity crowdfunding platform, with O'Leary's money and reputation of being a true shark, the entire industry got a boost and StartEngine's accelerated status, market share, and has grown into a significant and dynamic equity crowdfunding platform.

The fields of angel investing and crowdfunding have remained relatively obscure, a situation that is partly the result of the historical impact of the SEC (Securities and Exchange Commission) laws and regulations that once made issuers' solicitation for capital to investors illegal if they didn't already know them, *and* those potential investors were established millionaires. Founders could not 'general solicit' to the public for investment as they can today.

The Compassionate Capitalist Movement was born with the first book. **The Compassionate Capitalist Show** is a platform to amplify the message of how to create wealth as a successful business owner or as an investor in a successful business. A *Compassionate Capitalist* is someone who invests time, money, and resources into entrepreneurial endeavors to bring innovation to the market, create jobs, and generate wealth for all those involved. In a different way, "capitalist" is about making money; the compassion part is intending to make money not just by buying and selling, but by putting *it to work with impact.*

With this book, **"The Compassionalist"** is born. When I first set out to write a book about investing, my mission was clear: I wanted to educate and help everyday people, especially those from working-class backgrounds, access the world of investment opportunities previously locked away from them.

Too often, traditional investments, such as real estate, are reserved for those with large sums of capital. The reality is that many hardworking individuals don't have the accumulated financial holdings to participate in building a real estate investment portfolio, for their retirement or to create generational wealth.

Furthermore, most people haven't acquired the financial skills to analyze the merits and indicators of individual stocks. They lack the time to continually monitor the status of their stock investments and the volatility of the stock market. Their fear is valid; that their investments could collapse in value at any time due to external factors beyond their control.

Many people are working, day after day, and don't have the potential for "early retirement". Awareness of the potential in crowdfunding can be a catalyst for hope that they can lift themselves up by the bootstraps and get out of their financial 'rat-race'.

An AHA Moment – *Awareness* - Once they realize that both assets, private and public stocks, require time to research, manage, grow, and generate profit, each with its own risks, they will realize that the potential financial and emotional benefits from investing in entrepreneurs are so much greater than public stocks.

But how can we give them the skills, tools, and confidence to start and stay at it and build a profitable portfolio?

I wrote my book, *Inside Secrets to Angel Investing*, to help everyday people unlock the same opportunities once reserved for the wealthy elite. In the book, I dive deep into the strategies, tools, and insights that angel investors use. Although I touched on the history of crowdfunding in that book and explained how it allows anyone, regardless of their financial background, to participate in these high-growth, high-reward opportunities, I didn't provide the same level of 'how-to' for crowdfunding investing as I did with angel investing. Fans and subscribers to the Compassionate Capitalist Academy have been asking for an easy-to-follow guide specific to crowdfunding. This is that book.

This is written for those wealth-seeking Compassionate Capitalists – The Compassionalists that realize investing in 'the next big thing' no longer has to be an exclusive club for the rich. Anyone can participate and thrive with the proper knowledge and guidance; this book is intended to look specifically at crowdfunding investing so you can determine if this asset class is right for you and what the best practices are to build a profitable portfolio of investments. To help you understand the fundamentals of crowdfunding, the on-ramp to creating compounded wealth, I have created a fictional character, "Jane". Jane is a 'mashup' of those men and women I have met along the journey of life that I believe could leap the wealth gap, if they only knew they could, and how to do it with competence and confidence.

For the purpose of this book and the lessons contained within, Jane is a middle-aged, middle-class woman. Jane has her financial house in order. She "came into some money"

could be a performance bonus,

could be a sell-off of stocks because of the recent turmoil,

could be an inheritance,

could be a settlement,

could be a lottery win,

could be a sell-off of a rental that just wasn't working out,

could be a pool of funds from disciplined savings, trying to get enough to buy her first property, could be an underperforming retirement fund that could be diversified into higher yield crowdfund and angel investments…

You get the idea.

The source isn't as important. It is important to have access to capital to invest, optimism for the fun and challenge of the journey, and willingness to get started.

The Story of Jane

Jane is a Nurse Practitioner, a dedicated professional who works long hours caring for others and earns a good salary of $140,000 per year. But despite her hard work, she feels like she's constantly falling short in growing her wealth.

Jane has accumulated $40,000 over the years, but it doesn't feel like that is enough to make a real impact on the wealth she needs for her retirement and what she dreams of leaving her future generations. Even though she's been working hard, it feels like Jane is stuck in a system where the tools for wealth-building are out of her reach.

Jane's kids are out of college, so she doesn't have the added expense of helping them with tuition or living expenses. Her daughter is married, and she blessed Jane with her first grandson a couple of years ago. She also works in marketing. Jane's son is building a career in software engineering.

Jane knows she needs cash on hand in savings for those unexpected life events. She also knows you can't save your way to wealth, so she imagines the possibility of putting $20,000 to work in investments that give short-term income, with upside potential for bigger payback. Jane had heard that real estate was a great way to an income-producing investment that also builds long-term financial value; however, the reality is that with home prices continually rising, she can't afford to buy a fixer-upper property, much less start building a real estate portfolio leveraged with bank mortgages.

She had bought stocks now and then when she heard good news about the company or a tip from a Doctor at the hospital. The stock market may not be as costly as getting involved in real estate, but it was complicated to build a well-performing portfolio because so many factors that drove stocks up and down were beyond the company's control, and definitely beyond anything Jane could do other than try to predict the best time to sell or to buy.

She had heard a few people talk about investing in crypto, digital coins like Bitcoin. It seemed very promising. Celebrities were talking about and endorsing different platforms. She set up a digital wallet on one of the promos and took advantage of their $100 credit promo. Jane quickly realized that it was all about getting in on the ground floor because the value came in scarcity, not usually building anything.

Jane loved watching Shark Tank. She often wished she could have an idea that could become a profitable company. She never got an idea that she loved so much that she wanted to leave her job.   When she saw the headlines that one of the famous 'Sharks' had invested in a crowdfunding platform, she had an AHA moment:

If the super wealthy choose to invest in entrepreneurs' innovations because they believe they can make money at it, and most of the famous billionaire entrepreneurs became that because 'sharks' invested in them along the way and reaped those financial rewards too….hmmm

And anybody could do crowdfund investing and "Mr. Wonderful" thinks it is a good investment for him…. I should explore that possibility.

Jane considered the possibility of investing in small businesses and start-ups she believed in – to make money in a meaningful way. Rather than needing hundreds of thousands of dollars to purchase a rental property or a few stocks, she could invest small amounts, $1,000 to $2,000, into multiple companies. Different small businesses and startups that were solving different problems or having an impact that aligned with Jane's values.

Jane was excited about the potential of finding investment opportunities that align with her values, perhaps a healthcare start-up that aims to improve patient care or a tech company focused on sustainability. Over time, as these companies grow and expand, so will her investment. If the business succeeds, she succeeds as well.

Such is the power of crowdfunding investing. It allows people like Jane, those with the drive, vision, and desire, to leap the wealth gap without quitting their job to start a company or having hundreds of thousands of dollars to invest.

Crowdfund investors may participate in the same innovative opportunities as formerly reserved for the ultra-wealthy. By starting small, Jane could build a diverse portfolio, reduce risk, and share in the potential rewards when a company grows and succeeds.

The beauty of crowdfunding is that it democratizes access to capital for entrepreneurs and wealth-building tactics for all investors. High-growth investment opportunities are no longer accessible only to those already wealthy.

Whether you have $1,000, $10,000, or $100,000 per company to invest, crowdfunding allows you to invest in the companies and industries that excite you.

INSIDE SECRET #2

CROWDFUNDING OPENS UP A NEW WORLD OF POTENTIAL, ONE WHERE YOUR MONEY CAN WORK FOR YOU, JUST AS IT DOES FOR ANGEL INVESTORS WITH MILLIONS IN THE BANK. IT'S ABOUT GIVING EVERYDAY PEOPLE A CHANCE TO BE A PART OF SOMETHING BIGGER THAN THEMSELVES AND GROW THEIR WEALTH WHILE SUPPORTING INNOVATIVE COMPANIES THAT SOLVE REAL-WORLD PROBLEMS THEY CARE ABOUT.

Moreover, the opportunity doesn't just stop *at* making money; crowdfunding investing is also about supporting the growth of the economy and your local community; when you invest in local small businesses, you're contributing to the economic ecosystem by creating jobs, stimulating local economies, and driving innovation in areas you care about. You're not just a passive investor in a faceless corporation; you're a part of a larger mission, helping to bring new ideas to life and driving progress in ways that benefit everyone.

Let's face it: There's something profoundly fulfilling about knowing your money is working toward something positive, something that has the potential to change lives and solve problems. You might be thinking, "This sounds great, but where do I start?" That's what this book is here to help you with.

Successful crowdfunding is not just about throwing your money at any business that comes your way; it's about making informed, strategic decisions that align with your values and financial goals. As with successful angel investing, this kind of investing is about learning how to assess opportunities, mitigate risk, diversify your investments, and build a portfolio that gives you the best chance for success.

The legalization of equity-based crowdfunding investing has made it possible for anyone to participate. The days when you had to be an accredited investor or have a massive portfolio to get involved in high-growth businesses are gone. You can start investing as little as $500, sometimes even less, per company with the potential to change the world, grow your wealth, and take control of your financial future in a way that's accessible, manageable, and impactful. You're not just investing in a business; you're investing in a better future.

The economic imperative behind crowdfunding investing is clear here. In a world where traditional investments, like real estate and the stock market, are becoming increasingly difficult to access or are more volatile, crowdfunding offers a natural alternative. It's an opportunity to invest in companies that are solving problems and making a difference in the world. Unlike stocks or real estate, crowdfunding allows you to directly impact the growth of the business. You can be part of the next big success story, whether in your neighborhood or across the globe.

Working-class men and women often start side gigs or dream of leaving their unfulfilling jobs to start a business because they have heard that being a successful entrepreneur is the quickest way to create financial freedom. I'm here to show you that you don't have to incur all the risk of time and money starting and growing one business; you can put your money to work across multiple businesses, along with many other investors, where those founders are working harder than anyone to achieve their dreams. As one of their financial backers, you reap the same financial rewards without ALL the risk and investment of time.

INSIDE SECRET #3

*IF THE #1 WAY TO BECOME INDEPENDENTLY
WEALTHY IS TO BE A SUCCESSFUL
ENTREPRENEUR, THEN IT IS LOGICAL TO
CONCLUDE THE 2ND BEST WAY TO CREATE
GREAT WEALTH IS INVESTING IN MULTIPLE
BUSINESSES THAT SUCCEED AND EXIT RICH.*

RIGHT NOW, it is an excellent time for working-class people to step into the world of investing; no longer are the barriers to entry insurmountable, and with crowdfunding, you don't need to be a millionaire to invest. Crowdfund investing provides an opportunity to close the wealth gap and create a legacy for your family. With the economic uncertainty we face in the coming years, there is NO

BETTER TIME to create economic resilience by coming together to financially support the businesses we believe in so they can thrive. You only need capital, knowledge, and the drive to get started.

In this book, I'll introduce you to the fundamental principles that the successful angel investors I have worked with for so many years used to accumulate wealth. I'll use Jane's journey to walk you through the key stepping stones to help you understand the critical principles of crowdfunding investing, making intelligent investment decisions, and building a portfolio that aligns with your values and goals.

By the end of this book, you will have the knowledge you need to decide if this asset class is right for you. You will be invited to continue your educational journey in The Compassionalist Academy, where you will find the tools you need and gain the expertise to dive into the world of crowdfunding investing confidently. Whether you want to grow your wealth, support small businesses, or contribute to the economy's future, NOW is the time to take action. You're already at the table; you don't need an invitation. Just make your money work for you!

Ch. One: This Private Club is Public – And You are Invited

Investing in private companies has always been an appealing option for those who are willing to take on higher risks in exchange for the potential of higher rewards. However, this kind of investment has traditionally been a secret, something only the wealthy or well-connected were allowed to do. If you wanted to invest in a small business or start-up, you needed to be an "accredited investor", someone who meets specific financial requirements, like a high annual income or a significant net worth, meaning that the average person was excluded from opportunities to invest in companies that could potentially grow big and offer substantial financial returns.

The logic behind the restrictions was simple: startup companies are riskier, often small, have little to no track record, and could fail at any time. The equity investment into that kind of private company is illiquid, which means you can't just sell it like you can real estate or public stocks when it starts to lose value.

The rules around private stock investing were created after the Great Stock Market Crash that triggered the Great Depression. The industrialists who were investing in the modernization of America wanted to keep their business dealings private and out of the eyes of government regulators. The stock market crash caused widespread financial devastation for many people. In response, the SEC was created to help prevent such losses in the future. It established regulations aimed at protecting ordinary investors from the risks of losing their money in unproven speculative financial ventures. Therefore, the strategy for creating wealth by private investing was something only a select group of people, like venture capitalists and angel investors, could access. For decades, if you weren't invited into that exclusive circle, you couldn't just join in. However, all that changed in response to the second biggest financial market collapse, this time triggered by the 'real estate bubble' pop and the collapse of the financial market that led to the "Great Recession."

Evolution of Investment Opportunities

The SEC is the government body that regulates investments to ensure they are fair and safe. For many years, the SEC's Reg D provisions restricted private investments to accredited investors, rationalizing that if you had that much wealth, you had the financial acumen to manage and judge the risk of private venture investing. While intending to protect people from making risky decisions with their money, the actual impact was limiting capital available to entrepreneurs to fund innovation and create jobs.

Limiting startups' access to capital to only what comes from 'friends and family' that are millionaires, private angel investor clubs in major cities, or hiring costly licensed broker-dealers to raise capital from their high-net-worth clients stymied innovation and led to the high rate of bankruptcies typical in small businesses in their first five years of operation. Scarcity of capital for America's startups and growing small businesses has weakened America's stock market growth because 'going public' was not as common as it could or should be in a thriving and growing economy.

Then came the JOBS Act of 2012, which radically changed the investing landscape. It ushered in equity crowdfunding, which has led to more new startups than ever before (19 million in just the past three years), the concept of a "unicorn" company, and the longest sustained growth of the US Stock Market, reaching the highest levels in American history. This law opened the door for ordinary people, not just the wealthy, to invest in private companies. Suddenly, the "secret" of private investing was no longer reserved for the elite few. With the JOBS Act, anyone could potentially become an investor in a start-up, contributing to their growth and, hopefully, benefiting from their success.

Reasons for Approval of JOBS Act

The 2008 financial crisis was a significant turning point for many aspects of the economy. Small businesses, in particular, were hit hard. Many entrepreneurs struggled to get the funding to start or expand their businesses. Banks, the go-to source for business loans, became much more cautious after the crash, making it even harder for small businesses to get off the ground.

Reward-based crowdfunding has gained momentum in the 20 years since it started and has funded the development and commercialization of much of the technology we take for granted today. **Smartwatches, 3-D printing, Drones**, and even **VR headsets** first came to market as the general public invested money to get a reward, basically getting a product before it was generally available in stores. These early adopters got the benefit of a novel product, but when those companies raised venture capital and got acquired, all those early adopters had was *an obsolete product*. The $1000 they invested to get that product and help that company commercialize and get manufacturing up and running, that $1000 investment could have been worth $2000 or even $10,000, in the case of Oculus VR Headset when it was bought by Facebook years later.

At the same time, a societal shift was happening; people were becoming more interested in having a say in where their money went and how it could make a difference. Many saw the JOBS Act as a way to allow ordinary people, especially those who may have been excluded from wealth-building opportunities, to invest in new businesses and potentially share in the financial rewards. The JOBS Act became a way to solve two problems: giving small businesses a chance to grow by offering them new ways to raise capital and giving everyday people an opportunity to invest in ideas they believed in. It was a way of democratizing investment and creating a more inclusive financial system, especially when traditional business methods for getting capital seemed broken.

Impact of the Great Recession

The Great Recession began in 2007 and lasted into the following years, devastating the economy. The collapse of major financial institutions and the real estate market led to widespread job losses, bankruptcies, and a severe contraction in credit. Small businesses, the backbone of any economy, were particularly hard hit. Entrepreneurs with ideas for new products or services struggled to find the money they needed to bring those ideas to life. Once eager to lend to businesses, banks became fearful after the recession. They were unwilling to take risks on small businesses with limited performance history; this created a massive gap for entrepreneurs with great ideas, but who lacked the capital to make them a reality.

In 2007, Jane was still married. Their daughter was in business school. Their son was active in team travel sports and was about to graduate from high school. Even with their double income, she and her husband struggled to save and invest beyond a few stocks in an online account and put their max contribution to their 401K's. They were preparing to buy their first rental property and decided to wait and see if their son got a college scholarship when the collapse began.

For nearly 90 years, millionaires have built and multiplied their wealth by:

- Business Ownership, and/or
- Investing and owning a percentage of multiple other businesses.

There weren't enough investors before the Great Recession. Just like the availability of debt capital from the banks, private equity capital also became scarce. As the economy began to recover, the need for new ways to fund businesses became clear. Entrepreneurs needed a fresh way to access the capital they desperately needed to grow. The middle class needed a new way to accumulate wealth and overcome the loss of their financial nest egg due to the collapse of real estate values and the devastating crash of the stock market. The JOBS Act directly responded to those needs, solving two problems with one golden stone.

Jane saw the direct impact of bullish expectations of an investment in a "secure asset class" like real estate when her parents overextended themselves to build their real estate portfolio for monthly income. When the terms on their mortgages changed, and property taxes and insurance went up, suddenly one of their properties was costing money every month, and another went unoccupied for 6 months. They couldn't maintain them and couldn't sell them. The bank took them back. Her folks lost hundreds of thousands of dollars invested in the purchase, renovation, maintenance, and mortgage on the properties.

Introducing Equity Crowdfunding

Equity crowdfunding changed the game for entrepreneurs. Rather than relying on a few wealthy investors, entrepreneurs could now raise funds from many people, each investing small or large amounts, allowing start-ups and small businesses to access a much broader pool of capital. It democratized the investment process, allowing entrepreneurs to reach a wider audience without relying on traditional funding sources like angel investor networks and venture capitalists.

They could solicit investment capital from their customers, their community, their church, their alumnae and fraternal associations, organizations they are members of, and really anybody over the age of 18. Small businesses could now connect with a global pool of potential investors, allowing them to raise capital quickly and efficiently.

INSIDE SECRET: #4

THE PASSAGE OF THE JOBS ACT OF 2012 WAS A WIN-WIN: BUSINESSES COULD ACCESS THE FUNDS THEY NEEDED, AND INVESTORS HAD THE CHANCE TO GET IN ON THE GROUND FLOOR OF A PROMISING NEW VENTURE.

Status Quo Threat and Diverse Potential

As equity crowdfunding began to gain popularity, it created new opportunities for minority entrepreneurs, particularly African Americans and women, who had historically faced barriers to accessing capital. In the past, laws and financial practices had often worked against minority groups, making it harder for them to start and grow their businesses.

The rise of crowdfunding platforms allowed these entrepreneurs to bypass the traditional gatekeepers and access the funding they needed. Less than 2% of angel investor capital and less than 0.5% of venture capital goes to black and Latino founders. Female founders get about 2% of angel capital and venture capital, respectively, according to the latest reports.

INSIDE SECRET: #5

ALTHOUGH THE ALLOCATION OF CAPITAL FOR UNDERREPRESENTED FOUNDERS IS HIGHER THAN BEFORE 2020, TRENDS SHOW THAT THE AMOUNTS FROM ANGEL INVESTORS AND VENTURE CAPITAL ARE DECLINING AGAIN.

Not everyone welcomed this shift; some who had long benefited from the old system saw the rise of crowdfunding as a threat. The traditional financial system had been stacked in their favor, and now that entrepreneurs from underrepresented backgrounds were gaining access to funding, the status quo was being challenged. After all, they called the JOBS Act and the legalization of equity crowdfunding the great economic democratization of the capital markets. Since 2020, female founders have represented as much as 15% of the funded deals on REG CF (Regulation Crowdfunding) platforms, and POC founders represent as much as 28% of all Crowdfunded deals, according to Dealmaker.

What is a Gamble?

Why is it legal to gamble thousands of dollars in Las Vegas or buy lottery tickets every week (regardless of your income), but it is illegal to invest in an entrepreneur who could create jobs and contribute to economic growth? In some ways, investing in a start-up is much less risky than gambling, especially since entrepreneurs are actively trying to build something of value. Yet the law treated investment in businesses as off-limits for most people, while gambling was seen as an acceptable risk.

The rise of equity crowdfunding challenges this idea by offering everyday people a chance to invest in businesses they relate to and believe can make a real difference; this highlights the value of a more equitable system where anyone who wants to invest in an entrepreneur's success can do so regardless of their background or financial status.

Expanding Access to Capital and Wealth with the JOBS Act

The JOBS Act was pivotal in opening up equity crowdfunding to the public. The SEC set clear limits on how much a non-accredited investor could invest, subject to their income or net worth, trying to prevent people from investing more than they could afford to lose.

By easing the restrictions on raising capital, the JOBS Act also made it easier for entrepreneurs to get the funds they needed. They no longer had to go through the costly and time-consuming process of applying to pitch angel investor groups and pitch conferences, struggling to syndicate angel investor networks, and attracting venture capital as their only option for attracting capital. Instead, they could use crowdfunding platforms to connect with potential investors directly and start building their businesses more quickly.

INSIDE SECRET: #6

EQUITY CROWDFUNDING OPENS UP OPPORTUNITIES FOR BUSINESS OWNERS FROM ALL INDUSTRIES IN ALL STAGES OF GROWTH TO QUALIFY FOR CAPITAL IN DIFFERENT WAYS — REVENUE SHARE, DEBT, AND EQUITY. THAT MEANS INVESTORS OF ALL TYPES CAN REAP THE REWARDS OF POOLING THEIR FUNDS WITH OTHERS TO GET RETURNS IN THE WAYS THEY DESIRE BASED ON THEIR OWN FINANCIAL OBJECTIVES.

By 2017, when equity crowdfunding (REG CF) was fully authorized by the SEC, Jane was an empty nester. She was trying to find a new purpose, discover her passions, and was worried about her well-being in retirement. She believed there had to be a way to put the savings she had accumulated to work in a way that was fun AND financially and emotionally fulfilling.

Why Millionaires Choose Start-ups

But why are millionaires, who can invest in virtually anything, backing start-ups, small businesses, and ventures, often seen as risky? The answer lies in a deeper set of psychological and social motivations. When people invest in start-ups, they are not just looking for financial gain. They are fulfilling a range of personal needs that make such investments appealing. Let's look at our new investor, Jane, and how these soft benefits would impact her decision to put her money to work in private companies, entrepreneurs who are striving to solve problems that she understands and cares about.

Certainty

Millionaires often have diverse portfolios, including real estate, stocks, and other assets. Private company investments allow them to take control and diversify their holdings, providing more certainty in their overall financial picture. Jane would experience this if she targeted her investment dollars toward solutions she was certain would be useful in her experience as a healthcare worker. She could look for opportunities in bio-med and med techs, such as novel treatments for disease or functional products that improve the care of patients with limited mobility.

Uncertainty

While investing in start-ups is risky, uncertainty can be exciting for some investors. There's a rush in betting on a business that could go big. Although Jane may experience uncertainty in her job as a result of the care of her patients, this is a different type of uncertainty because if she has done her due diligence, she may have confidence in the success of the company she invests in, but uncertainty about how big that success would be. Uncertainty, in this case, is the anticipation of the impact her money will have and her return on investment.

Significance

By investing in a business, millionaires feel they are contributing to something meaningful. They are helping a company grow, shape its future, and make an impact. Whether Jane uses her vocational experience to discern the need for a product or solution in healthcare, she will also draw from her other interests, perhaps from other studies or hobbies. She feels good about the impact her money will have as she joins other investors to financially back a company, and she knows that when the company she invests in succeeds, the significance of their contribution to improving people's lives, jobs created, and wealth spread to employees, vendors, and investors will be rewarding.

Connection

Many investors feel a personal connection to the entrepreneurs they back. These connections feel more personal, whether it's a shared vision or a belief in the business's mission. When Jane finds a company that is doing something she really believes in because she understands the problem being solved, she will feel a connection to that company, even if she never meets the CEO.

Growth

Start-ups embody innovation and progress. Investors are attracted to businesses pushing the boundaries of what's possible, whether it's through new technology or social impact. Once Jane makes her investment and starts to get reports of the progress the company is making, perhaps by seeing their name in the news, she will feel the joy of watching them grow. Think of the joy you feel when the seeds you planted peek above ground and grow, or when you see a baby take its first steps. That is how angel investors feel about their investments. Crowdfunding investing is just another version of angel investing.

Contribution

Finally, investing in start-ups allows millionaires to contribute to job creation, innovation, and broader economic growth. It gives them a sense of purpose beyond just making money. They feel investing this way can leave a legacy that they contributed to making the world a better place. Jane, as most of us do, cares about the future we leave for our children and grandchildren. By investing in entrepreneurs, whether in the startup or growth stage, Jane knows she is contributing to the economy with that company's tangible success. Additionally, as their solution, their innovation, is adopted and begins to transform an industry or solve a problem that people have experienced for a long time, particularly in healthcare, she knows her dollars will have a lasting contribution to the betterment of future generations.

INSIDE SECRET: #7

OVER THE DECADES, I HAVE BEEN INVOLVED WITH CULTIVATING RELATIONSHIPS WITH MILLIONAIRES WHO ARE ANGEL INVESTORS, AND ONE THING HAS BEEN CLEAR TO ME. THEY STAND APART FROM OTHER TRADITIONAL INVESTORS BECAUSE THEY CHOOSE TO INVEST IN A WAY THAT NOT ONLY COMPOUNDS THEIR WEALTH BUT ALSO MAKES THEM FEEL GOOD ABOUT IT. WHEN I LOOKED UP THE HIERARCHY OF NEEDS, I UNDERSTOOD THE MOTIVATION THAT WAS NOT JUST ABOUT MAKING MORE MONEY (CAPITALIST), BUT ALSO ABOUT THE IMPACT THEIR MONEY COULD HAVE ON SOLVING PROBLEMS (COMPASSIONATE)

Crowdfunding and the Future of Investing

The JOBS Act has opened the door for millions of people to participate in funding the next generation of start-ups and small businesses. As crowdfunding grows, it's likely to reshape the financial landscape, making it more inclusive and accessible. Entrepreneurs now have new ways to raise capital, and investors have new ways to share in the success of businesses that could transform the world and make crowdfunding an exciting new chapter in the history of investing, one where everyone, *and frankly, anyone*, can get involved.

Ch. Two: Understanding How It Works

Understanding how a crowdfunding investment works is crucial for anyone considering this form of investment. Unlike traditional investing methods, such as transactions between other investors buying and selling stocks in publicly traded companies or buying and selling real estate, crowdfunding offers a different model. Many people invest varying amounts of capital, from small to large amounts, and that capital is pooled together to fund startups, small businesses, or even large-scale projects.

Crowdfunding has grown rapidly in recent years, reshaping how we invest and how startups and growth-stage companies get funded. By understanding how these investments operate, potential investors can make informed decisions, assess risks effectively, and capitalize on opportunities that were once only available to a select few. It allows individuals to invest in various industries and businesses, ranging from tech startups to growing "main street" small businesses, and even late-stage businesses preparing for exit. Access to these opportunities, because of the authorization of Equity crowdfunding, removes the barriers to entry that traditionally kept small investors out of these opportunities.

However, the underlying nature of crowdfunding, where many individuals contribute smaller amounts than, say, traditional 'business' angel investors and venture capitalists, can be complex. It is still a private transaction regulated by the SEC, and therefore, there are laws governing how companies raise capital and the consequences for those who don't follow the rules.

Different types of crowdfunding, such as equity, debt, or revenue-sharing, each come with distinct risks, rewards, and legal requirements. The way an investor gets their return may be packaged in these different ways, while the underlying structure adheres to the four types of equity crowdfunding authorized by the JOBS Act. It is essential to understand how each investment type works, the protective measures in place, and the potential returns to succeed in crowdfunding as an investor.

Understanding the various crowdfunding investment methods helps investors familiarize themselves with the platforms facilitating these transactions. These platforms offer access to investment opportunities but also ensure that these opportunities comply with legal regulations, offer transparency, and are securely managed. Knowing how crowdfunding investments work enables investors to confidently participate in projects that align with their values, financial goals, and risk tolerance.

Whether you're considering becoming a part of a growing innovative startup, contributing to community-based Main Street business opportunities or real estate development projects, or lending funds through debt-based models, understanding the mechanics of crowdfunding investments ensures that you are making wise, informed choices that support both your financial objectives and the success of the businesses you invest in. Through crowdfunding, people from all walks of life can contribute to and benefit from the success of startups, real estate ventures, small businesses, and even large-scale corporate expansion initiatives.

When Jane decided she wanted to explore crowdfunding as a wealth creation strategy, she was both enthusiastic about the variety of opportunities, but also anxious about how to get started. She very much wanted to get started right and avoid investments she would look

back on and think: "That was stupid, I should have known better."

How Crowdfunding Investments Work

Investing through crowdfunding differs significantly from traditional investments like stocks or bonds. It offers various investment models, including equity-based, debt-based, and revenue-share crowdfunding. Each type of investment has its rewards, risks, and expectations, so investors must understand how each model works. A well-diversified equity investment portfolio should include different industries, stages, and structures of the offerings.

Equity-based Crowdfunding

First, you must understand that investing in private companies is similar to investing in the stock market because the stock is the equity. What the investor owns is the same. They differ in that one is bought and sold to another investor in a public market. The other is bought from the company in a private equity investment as an angel/crowdfund investor. In equity crowdfunding, as with angel investing, investors purchase shares in a company, giving them ownership of the business. Equity crowdfunding is appealing because it offers the potential for substantial returns if the business grows and thrives.

How much money is returned on investment will depend on the stage and value of the stock equity being purchased. The earlier the stage of the company seeking investment, the greater the potential return. However, the earlier the stage, the greater the risk because many startups fail. Equity crowdfunding allows small investors to get involved with businesses early, investing smaller amounts initially, so the loss may not be significant, but with the potential to lead to significant financial rewards if the company succeeds.

INSIDE SECRET: #9

A PRINCIPLE USED BY SAVVY, EXPERIENCED ANGEL INVESTORS CAN ALSO BE USED BY CROWDFUNDING INVESTORS. THE EARLIER THE STAGE OF THE COMPANY, THE GREATER THE RISK. THEREFORE, THEY START SMALL AND INVEST MORE AS THE COMPANY PROVES THEY HAVE THE ABILITY TO REACH MILESTONES AND SCALE.

Later-stage companies, those with an operating history that shows their ability to make a profit and have been profitable for years, also need more capital than they can get from other traditional lending sources. Investors can match the debt they qualify for so that they accelerate their growth to launch a new product, expand production, or open another location. The equity they offer will have a higher value, so the return will be less than that of a startup, but the risk is also significantly lower. The return on a growth-stage company will still be more than buying stock of that company after it goes public.

Debt-based Crowdfunding (Lending)

Debt-based crowdfunding involves lending money to businesses with the expectation of repayment over time with interest. This model is less risky than equity-based crowdfunding, as investors are not reliant on the company's sizable growth and subsequent exit for a return. Instead, they receive fixed payments according to the terms of the loan agreement.

Similar to a loan request from a bank, companies seeking crowd-sourced debt must undergo an evaluation and underwriting process to ensure they have the operational wherewithal to repay the loan. While the debt-based crowdfunding model may not offer the same high potential rewards as equity crowdfunding, it provides more predictable returns. Those returns are typically better than stock annuities and interest on savings or CDs. The investor trades the high return of a company's shares, increasing in value for the security of a predictable return of a debt-based offering.

INSIDE SECRET: #10

*A GOOD ANGEL OR CROWDFUNDING
STRATEGY IS TO BUILD A DIVERSE
PORTFOLIO OF COMPANIES FROM
DIFFERENT INDUSTRIES AT DIFFERENT
STAGES; AND THAT SEEK CAPITAL THAT WILL
PAY OUT RETURNS IN DIFFERENT WAYS.*

Revenue-sharing Crowdfunding

Revenue-sharing crowdfunding is a hybrid model where investors receive a percentage of a company's future revenue. This model allows investors to earn ongoing returns as the company generates more revenue. Unlike equity crowdfunding, investors in revenue-sharing models do not own shares in the company but instead participate in the profits generated by its success. Companies may choose to offer revenue-based returns to their investors rather than equity because they are building a business, and they plan to keep longer than equity-based investors want to wait for their return.

As Jane develops her strategy to build a profitable investment portfolio, she likes the idea of starting with debt and/or revenue share opportunities so she can see modest returns on her initial investments. This approach also grants her time and peace of mind as she searches for companies offering solutions to solve an industry problem that she cares about.

INSIDE SECRET: #11

IN THE COMPASSIONALIST ACADEMY TRAINING PLATFORM, I TEACH THE "ANGEL PROFITABILITY BLUEPRINT" FOR BUILDING A STRONG, DIVERSIFIED PORTFOLIO OF INVESTMENTS. WE BREAK DOWN HOW TO TAKE THE CAPITAL YOU HAVE AVAILABLE AND SPREAD THAT ACROSS 10 INVESTMENTS OVER 2-3 YEARS TO CREATE MODEST RETURNS WITHIN 6 MONTHS AND LONG-TERM, LARGE RETURNS WITH RESILIENCE AGAINST MARKET SHIFTS.

Real Estate and Large-Scale Crowdfunding

Traditionally, real estate investments were made by institutional investors or individuals with significant capital, whether investing in commercial properties, long-term and short-term rentals, or significant mixed-use and residential developments. One of the most notable evolutions in crowdfunding has been the rise of real estate crowdfunding. Crowdfunding platforms like Fundrise and RealtyMogul have radically altered this landscape, allowing individuals to pool their resources and invest in high-value real estate projects.

Furthermore, crowdfunding platforms typically offer **debt-based crowdfunding** or **revenue-sharing models**. In **a debt-based model**, investors lend money to a company and receive periodic interest and principal payments. In real estate revenue-share models (the terms vary and need to be studied carefully), investors may receive their payout in a share of the rental income until a guaranteed ROI is reached or there is a sell-off of the property or equity. Real estate crowdfunding opportunities offer an accessible way for smaller investors to diversify their portfolios with real estate they could never afford on their own in the current inflated market value and high interest rates. In some ways, it can be the best of both worlds. Crowdfund investors can potentially earn returns from what has long been considered a typically profitable sector, real estate. Crowdfunding has also opened exclusive markets to everyday investors, allowing them to diversify their portfolios and support community development, particularly in real estate, that otherwise would be price prohibitive.

As Jane began to explore the various types of offerings available through crowdfunding, she was pleased to learn she could be a minority investor in a large urban renewal project in her hometown. Jane felt good about being able to put a portion of her investment pool of funds to work with a clear economic impact. She learned a new term along the way: "Special Purpose Vehicle". When she first learned her investment would be combined with many other co-investors in an SPV. (Not a road trip to visit the property, although she certainly was looking forward to taking her mom by the construction site the next time she went "home" for a visit). The SPV is a legal entity that puts

all those investors into one shareholder group with specific terms, rights, and protections.

Role of Crowdfunding Platforms

Crowdfunding platforms are vital in connecting businesses with potential investors, functioning as intermediaries that provide the necessary infrastructure to raise funds from a broad pool of backers. Platforms such as Kickstarter and Indiegogo offer reward-based crowdfunding. On the other hand, Republic, StartEngine, Wefunder in the US, and Crowdcube in Europe offer equity-based crowdfunding under the provisions of the Regulation Crowdfunding (REG CF).

Companies raising capital under other equity crowdfunding provisions (Reg D 506c and Reg A+) may look to StartEngine, Republic, MicroVentures, and others that are licensed as Broker-Dealer service providers. Indiegogo has teamed up with StartEngine to offer reward-based offers leading into or alongside REG CF, Reg A+, and Reg D 506c equity-based campaigns for their entrepreneurs.

Although issuers are free to structure their offering as equity or debt, platforms like StartEngine, Republic, MicroVentures, and Wefunder are primarily centered around equity investments, allowing investors to own a portion of the companies they invest in. Honeycomb and SMBX are structured as equity crowdfunding platforms, but their issuers do so by issuing notes as fixed-term debt rather than equity.

Crowdfunding platforms are not just about raising capital; they also provide businesses with a way to build a community. Businesses can strengthen brand loyalty and gain valuable market insights by engaging investors, who may also become potential customers.

Often, you will find companies that are established, even venture capital-backed, raising capital on a crowdfunding platform to raise a little capital and grow the number of total investors to better position themselves for an IPO. These platforms ensure that the entire crowdfunding process remains secure, transparent, and compliant with laws, further protecting the interests of investors and entrepreneurs.

INSIDE SECRET: #12

IT IS IMPORTANT TO NOTE THAT BY LAW, THE REG CF PLATFORMS ARE NOT ALLOWED TO SOLICIT CAPITAL FROM THE GENERAL PUBLIC FOR THE OFFERORS ON THEIR PLATFORM. THEY HAVE A COMMUNITY THEY HAVE DEVELOPED OVER TIME THAT SUBSCRIBES TO THEIR PLATFORMS. THE ISSUERS ARE RESPONSIBLE FOR GENERATING INTEREST IN THEIR OFFERINGS THROUGH THEIR OWN CONNECTIONS, CUSTOMERS, FOLLOWERS, AND SUBSCRIBERS, AS WELL AS THROUGH ADVERTISING. REG CF PLATFORMS ARE AUTHORIZED TO SEND OUT EMAILS TO THEIR OWN DATABASE ON BEHALF OF ISSUERS WHEN KEY MILESTONES AND THRESHOLDS ARE MET, SUCH AS: QUALIFIED OFFERING, INVESTMENT CAPITAL THRESHOLDS ARE REACHED, WHEN THEY TARGET FOR THE ROUND ARE CLOSE TO BEING MET, AND WHEN THEY ARE REACHED. THEY CAN ALSO SHARE INFORMATION ABOUT WHETHER THE COMPANY IS CONDUCTING AN INVESTOR WEBINAR.

Community-Based Investing

Just before the JOBS Act was enacted by Congress in 2012, Georgia and Indiana passed legislation that made it legal for companies domiciled in their state to 'general solicit' from the investors residing in their state. This ability was authorized under a provision called "Intrastate Exemption." It was a big deal at the time because it separated the regulatory authority from the Federal Government and empowered the state to create a catalyst for economic development in their communities. The SEC ultimately recognized this and allowed the long-standing Reg D 504 provision to be used, which allowed states to authorize up to $5M in capital to be raised this way.

What this means for startups, small business owners, and established companies seeking to expand is that they can solicit investment from their customers, friends, and acquaintances, and organizations in their community, without the cost and complexity of launching a capital raise effort common to the other types of equity crowdfunding. All the elements of being "investable" need to be there.

With Intrastate Exemption, the opportunity to create 'investor clubs' by association for wealth creation for both sides of the table – the investors and the companies is numerous:

- Universities cultivating innovation on their campuses with comprehensive programs to develop entrepreneurial leaders can solicit their alumnae living in that state. The students and grads can solicit their fraternity and sorority chapters in that state.

- Chamber of Commerce groups can grow their local economy by showcasing members that are expanding and encouraging other members to invest in those qualified companies.

- Organizations established to create Economic Opportunity and Empowerment for diverse business owners can reach out to their community and members to invest in the startups they are incubating and the established companies they are accelerating.

- Churches can build a financially more resilient community by creating opportunities for business owners who are members to present to other members about their opportunity.

- A business owner who wants to open up a second location can invite their customers to invest and share in their revenue as they grow their business.

Intrastate Exemption is like the new "shop local" but with "invest local." Startups, particularly diverse founders, struggle to get the capital to build their first product prototype so that they can qualify for angel investor capital. Small business owners struggle to qualify for capital from lenders beyond the value of the hard assets or current cash flow to invest in the products, services, and people they need to scale. Tapping the extra money sitting on the sidelines, in their 'neighbours' saving and checking accounts, is a great way to create a win-win-win: Businesses thrive and buy more products and services, jobs are created within the community, and the local investors get to share in that success too.

Understanding Investor Protections

While crowdfunding offers exciting opportunities, investors must be aware of the various protections to safeguard their investments, so that they are aware of their own responsibilities in evaluating the risk/reward ratio of an offer. Protective measures can vary depending on the type of crowdfunding involved, whether it's equity-based, debt-based, or revenue-sharing. Laws are in place that aim to enhance transparency and reduce risks, but these are still private transactions and do not have the same requirement for disclosure as public companies.

For example, under REG CF and Reg A+, companies raising funds must provide detailed financial disclosures. These financial disclosures allow investors to assess the risks and make informed decisions before committing money. The SEC regulates this process, ensuring companies adhere to legal frameworks that protect investors. The level of disclosure and review by accountants varies by offering, but it is reassuring to know that there is a requirement. There is no legal requirement for such financial disclosure with traditional angel investing. Experienced angel investors have learned to conduct due diligence and ask for information not readily available in the public documents.

All equity investment opportunities must include clear information about the risks involved. REG D offerings are typically shared in a document called the Private Placement Memorandum. For REG CF, the risks are outlined in Form C, which is filed with the SEC. Similarly, Reg A+ offerings must include their risk factors and audited financials in their registration.

Platforms that offer equity crowdfunding under REG CF are regulated by FINRA, the same organization that oversees financial professionals like brokers/dealers and financial planners. This provides an extra layer of protection for investors. One of the key protections is the "Bad Actor" rule, which prevents individuals with a history of investment fraud or legal issues from holding executive and fiduciary positions in any company leading a crowdfunding campaign.

Additionally, many crowdfunding platforms offer services for resolving disputes and providing regular financial updates, adding transparency and accountability. Some platforms even offer return guarantees for specific investments, although these come with their own set of conditions. These protections and disclosures help create a safer environment for investors. However, it's crucial to understand that risks like fraud or market fluctuations can still be present, making it imperative for investors to conduct thorough research and remain cautious about potential scams.

Benefits of Crowdfunding

One of the most prominent benefits of crowdfunding is the opportunity to diversify investment portfolios. In traditional investment models, small investors were often limited to stocks of publicly traded companies or mutual funds. With crowdfunding, individuals can invest with impact in a wide range of industries, from emerging technology companies and green energy startups to local restaurants, small manufacturers, and agriculture businesses they admire. This broader range of investment opportunities gives investors more control over where their money goes, allowing them to align their investments with personal values, whether supporting eco-friendly initiatives or local businesses.

As Jane started to think about the kind of companies and opportunities she wanted to invest in, she was open to investing in local businesses but wasn't sure how to identify them. She also wanted to find companies that were working on the problems she cared about, from her work in health care and innovation, addressing aspects of climate change. Jane was excited to see the vast variety of companies raising capital as she signed up and subscribed to the different crowdfunding platforms.

Lower Barriers to Entry

Crowdfunding has changed the way people invest by making it easier for more people to get involved. In the past, venture capital and angel investing were mainly for wealthy individuals who could afford to put large amounts of money into businesses.

To be an "accredited investor," someone had to meet certain requirements. For example, they needed to make at least $200,000 a year (or $300,000 with a spouse) for the last two years and expect to make the same amount this year. Alternatively, they can qualify if they have a net worth of over $1 million, not counting the value of their home. There are also new provisions for 'sophisticated investors' to qualify based on their knowledge and experience in financial matters to understand the risks and merits of a founder's offering.

Thanks to equity crowdfunding, which opened up the opportunity for 'non-accredited' investors to invest in entrepreneurs' endeavors, more people can now invest in startups and small businesses, creating new opportunities that were once limited to the wealthy. Equity crowdfunding, by contrast, allows individuals to invest small amounts, often as low as $500 or $1,000, which opens up these investment opportunities to a much larger pool of people. This lower barrier to entry makes it easier for those without significant wealth to engage with the investment process, enabling them to take part in opportunities they may have otherwise been excluded from.

Risk Mitigation Through Collective Investment

Another significant advantage of crowdfunding is the distribution of risk. In traditional angel investments, a wealthy investor might risk a substantial sum when investing in a business. If that business fails, the investor's loss is much larger. The national average that a traditional Angel invests is $25,000. Angel investors co-invest with other angel investors to pool their funds to leverage many hundreds of thousands of dollars, even millions of dollars. Similarly, in crowdfunding, this risk is spread across many people, each with the option to contribute the investment capital they are comfortable with investing.

INSIDE SECRET: #13

RELATIVELY SPEAKING, AS A PERCENTAGE OF WEALTH AND LIQUIDITY, A $2000 INVESTMENT FROM A NON-ACCREDITED, NON-MILLIONAIRE MAY CARRY THE SAME WEIGHT AS AN ACCREDITED INVESTOR MAKING A $20,000 INVESTMENT. THE RESULTING RETURN ON THAT INVESTMENT COULD ALSO HAVE AS MUCH IMPACT ON THE GROWTH OF WEALTH AS THE OVERALL HOUSEHOLD INCOME. THAT IS WHY EQUITY CROWDFUNDING HAS BEEN CALLED "THE GREAT ECONOMIC DEMOCRATIZATION OF THE CAPITAL MARKETS". IT IS PROVING TO BE THE SINGLE GREATEST WAY TO LEAP THE WEALTH GAP IN A SYSTEMATIC, THOUGHTFUL, AND IMPACTFUL WAY.

Depending on the type of offering and stage, the amount of the ask will vary. Typically, a startup may initially raise a few hundred thousand and raise more in subsequent rounds after accomplishing significant milestones with that money. A later-stage company may seek a wide range from $20M to $75M from small crowdfunding investors up to large institutional investors.

The amount invested should always be within the risk parameter of what the investor can lose without causing hardship to them or their family. By pooling the investment from many investors, the company effectively reduces the financial exposure for each investor, lowering the potential loss impact. Many crowdfunding platforms even feature milestone-based funding, where businesses must meet pre-determined goals before receiving the funds. Milestone-based funding is an additional safeguard, ensuring the business progresses before receiving full funding.

Once Jane figured out that she was not 'alone' in helping entrepreneurs with their financial needs to get to market and grow, she felt empowered. While she worked hard at her job, the entrepreneurs she invested in were working even harder to fulfill their own dreams. She had often wondered about quitting her job to go start a business but never felt confident about any of her ideas. She enjoyed being a nurse, having a steady income, and having guaranteed health benefits. With equity crowdfunding, she could put her money to work for her and share in the success of the businesses she invested in.

Types of Equity Crowdfunding

Equity crowdfunding is a modern way for businesses to raise money by offering a share of ownership to many people from all walks of life and incomes, often called investors or backers. This process differs from traditional private equity fundraising, where businesses must rely on wealthy high-net-worth individuals or big institutions to invest large sums of money. With equity crowdfunding, investors can participate by putting in smaller amounts. Crowdfunding, similar to traditional private equity capital formation, is subject to strict rules and regulations that are in place to protect investors and companies. There are four primary types of equity crowdfunding, each with its own set of rules:

- Intrastate Exemption,
- REG CF,
- REG D 506C, and
- REG A+.

1. Intrastate Exemption

The Intrastate Exemption is the most localized and generally considered the simplest form of equity crowdfunding. It allows businesses to raise money from investors residing in the same state. This option is perfect for companies that want to raise funds from their local community without dealing with the complicated rules set by the federal government. The goal is to make it easier for businesses to get funding from people already familiar with their products or services.

Key Features:

Local Only: Only people who live in the same state as the business can invest. For example, if a restaurant in Texas wants to raise money, only people who live in Texas can invest.

State-Level Rules: Each state has its own rules on how crowdfunding can be done. Businesses need to follow specific guidelines that apply only to that state, making it easier to comply with laws at a local level. The variations between states could be how the company qualifies, who can invest, and/or how much can be raised. Although the SEC has authorized up to $5 million for accredited and unaccredited investors, not every state has implemented its program in the same way. As of this publication, 34 states and the District of Columbia have enacted some form of intrastate crowdfunding laws.

Community Engagement: It can help businesses build a strong connection with their community by allowing local customers or supporters to invest in the company, potentially increasing customer loyalty and trust.

Pros: It's easier and cheaper for businesses to raise money since they don't have to deal with complex federal laws. It's also an excellent way for businesses to get local 'friendly' financial support. They typically have a built-in potential pool of investors from their customers and community organizations they are members of.

Cons: The main limitation is that the investors must be from the same state, restricting the number of potential investors, which could make it harder for businesses to raise large sums unless they use Intrastate Exemption as a steppingstone to a larger national capital raise.

2. REG CF (Regulation Crowdfunding)

REG CF, or Regulation Crowdfunding, is a more open way to raise money that allows companies to raise up to $5 million each year. REG CF differs from the intrastate exemption because, by statute, anyone can invest, whether wealthy (accredited investors) or not (unaccredited investors), making it much more accessible for everyday people across America to invest in startups, small businesses, or other projects.

Key Features:

Accessible to Everyone: REG CF allows anyone to invest. However, it limits how much unaccredited investors can invest based on their income or net worth, helping prevent people from overinvesting or risking money they can't afford to lose.

Investment Limits for Unaccredited Investors: Unaccredited investors (regular people) have a limit on how much they can invest each year. This limit is based on their income or net worth, which is justified in the SEC's role to protect investors.

Although the government doesn't limit how much money people can spend on the lottery every month or how much they risk on gambling excursions, they do have caps on how much an 'unaccredited' investor may invest in a specific opportunity and the total amount of investments in a year. Current law for non-accredited investors investing in equity crowdfunding offers allows them to invest a maximum of $2000 in a single issue, and $10,000 total in a year.

$5 Million Cap: The most a company can raise under REG CF is $5 million yearly, making it ideal for small businesses or startups looking for funding. Most startup companies raise significantly less to start because they have to balance the ask with the value of the company.

Disclosure and Transparency: Companies must provide detailed information about their business, including financials and potential risks, to help investors make informed decisions. REG CF issuers file a Form C with the SEC, and it must be updated regularly to reflect any changes to the offer, the value of the company, and shifts in strategy.

Pros: REG CF allows anyone to invest, making it possible for ordinary people to get involved in the growth of businesses. The combination of the SEC filing requirements and the platform FINRA requirements seeks to help protect investors by requiring full transparency.

Another unique feature of REG CF is that the equity capital raised is subject to the same milestones as reward-based crowdfunding. Companies declare how much they intend to raise and set milestones. They do not receive their capital until the milestone has been met. Investors' investment is held in escrow until the milestone is reached. If it isn't reached, meaning the company did not raise enough capital to do what they intended with the money, the money is returned to the investors.

Cons: It is important to note that although FINRA regulates REG CF platforms and is responsible for making sure the correct paperwork is filed with the SEC, they ARE NOT responsible for validating if the business can succeed, nor do they endorse or recommend investments on their platform.

As with other private equity investment solicitations, no one is 'vouching' for the company. It is incumbent on the investor to do their own due diligence and assess the risk vs potential reward of the return on investment when choosing one investment over another. That responsibility rightly belongs to the backers investing capital into the deal.

3. REG D 506C (Rule 506(c) of Regulation D)

REG D 506C is a crowdfunding option only available to accredited investors wealthy enough to meet specific income or net worth requirements. This type of crowdfunding is similar to all the other manners in which issuers can 'generally solicit' for investors, because it allows companies to advertise their fundraising efforts to reach a wider audience nationwide, publicly, like a public stock company. Although issuers are not required to list on a portal or hire a broker-dealer, they must have a mechanism to validate that only accredited investors participate in their offering.

Both offering provisions for raising capital under Reg D 506B and 506C must file a FORM D with the SEC. Issuers under Reg D 506B file it following their first investment of capital, while Reg D 506C files their FORM D before they start soliciting for capital.

Key Features:

Accredited Investors Only: Only people who meet the SEC's definition of an accredited investor can invest. These are individuals with a high income or a considerable net worth (earned income over $200,000 a year or a net worth of over $1 million, not including the primary residence).

High net-worth (HNW) accredited investors found in angel clubs and through traditional capital raise practices under the legacy exemptions of Reg D 506B, only need to sign an 'Investor Questionnaire' that self-certifies their wealth status to qualify for this type of investment. A key difference between Reg D 506B and Reg D 506C is that 506B allows for up to 35 unaccredited investors to participate. Companies raising capital will use this exception to document the services paid through equity, as contractors developing their product or building their website may take payment in the form of equity and may not be accredited.

Sophisticated Investor Provision: An individual with enough experience, knowledge, and financial resources to evaluate the merit of the deal and understand the risks involved in an investment may invest as if they were accredited. This means they can access investment opportunities that are not available to the general public, like certain private or equity crowdfunding campaigns. In the U.S., the definition of a "sophisticated investor" includes people who may not meet specific income or net worth requirements. Other countries have their own definitions, but the idea is the same: these investors are skilled enough to make decisions without needing as much regulatory protection.

Public Advertising: Fundamental to crowdfunding, businesses can publicly advertise their investment offers, allowing companies to utilize social media, websites, and other marketing tools to get the word out about their fundraising campaign. This differs from the 'sister' to REG D 506C, which is REG D 506B, which is how traditional angels invest in private companies. Companies raising capital under REG D 506B must follow the original Securities laws of the 1930s and not solicit the public for investment. They must know their investors in advance, apply for investment to angel investor groups, or work through a licensed dealer–broker.

No Fundraising Limit: One of the most significant advantages of REG D 506C is that there's no limit to how much a company can raise. If a company wants to raise millions or even tens of millions, this option allows them to do so.

Investor Verification: Companies must verify that their investors are accredited, which involves checking financial documents to prove they meet the criteria, adding a layer of security for the company, and helping ensure only qualified investors are involved. Their investors can optionally provide a certified letter from a licensed service provider, like an accountant, lawyer, or financial planner, that they are accredited, or they can pay a service to 'vouch' that they are accredited because they have provided the necessary evidential documentation.

Pros: Businesses can raise as much money as they need, and the ability to advertise publicly allows them to reach a broad audience. It's also beneficial for larger, more established companies that require significant capital. This method also opens doors to high-net-worth individuals and family offices that may not be part of traditional angel groups.

Cons: Only wealthy, accredited investors can participate, excluding many potential investors, especially those who may be interested but do not meet the strict criteria. Some traditional angel investors feel the financial disclosure aspect of qualifying for this type of investment is intrusive and do not want to go through the verification process unless they are highly motivated. Active accredited investors will subscribe to a 3rd party service that confidentially and securely stores their verification data and submits on their behalf to Reg D 506C issuers.

Jane began to understand that she needed to stay within the provisions of qualification as a 'non-accredited' investor, and as a new investor, she was not a 'sophisticated investor." She was happy she could start small and develop her skills of discernment and financial risk assessment. She made a goal to grow into being considered a 'sophisticated investor' as she became more confident and competent with training, mentoring, and practice. Jane believed she could begin to create wealth by investing in entrepreneurs who had previously eluded her in her career and other investments, and with time, she would become a qualified accredited investor.

4. REG A+ (Regulation A+)

REG A+ is the most flexible crowdfunding model, allowing companies to raise up to $75 million annually from accredited and non-accredited investors. This makes it an excellent option for companies looking to raise a large amount of money. It is ideal for businesses that are a little further along and ready for more serious investment.

Frequently, companies raising capital under REG A+ have raised an early seed round and even a Series A round, but for a variety of reasons, they have not gone on to raise venture capital. They use REG A+ as a means to raise capital to boost their business with new products and new markets. They can solicit their customers, raise brand awareness that attracts new customers along with investors, create new revenue streams, and prepare for exit through acquisition or filing to be public on stock exchanges like NASDAQ Small Cap.

Key Features:

Large Fundraising Limits: Since REG A+ is typically used by established companies seeking growth capital, there is often a perceived lower risk compared to startups or early-stage ventures. The reporting requirements offer more transparency than other private offerings. With the ability to raise up to $75 million annually, REG A+ allows companies to secure substantial funding for growth, new products, or large-scale projects, which can be a sign of a company's ambition and stability. This combination of transparency, lower perceived risk, and substantial fundraising potential makes REG A+ an attractive option for investors looking to back companies with a solid foundation and significant growth opportunities.

Two Fundraising Tiers: REG A+ (Tier II of the long-standing REG A provision) was introduced as part of the JOBS Act, which aimed to simplify the fundraising process for businesses. Before REG A+ was established, there was simply Regulation A that offered an exemption for small stock issuance, which was even called a 'mini-IPO,' which is how REG A+ is referred to today. However, the maximum amount that could be raised under the provision was $5M and was used infrequently. It allowed for 'testing the waters' with potential investors before filing in the state where the offering would be issued, a process that was costly and time-consuming. That all changed with the JOBS Act of 2012.

Today, REG A offers two main fundraising tiers:

- **Tier 1:** Companies can raise up to $20 million annually, with fewer disclosure requirements, making it a less expensive and complex option for smaller or early-stage companies. However, it still requires filing with each state, which adds a layer of cost and additional regulatory filings. Tier 1 is limited to accredited investors. Tier 1 must raise capital through a broker/dealer and cannot solicit from the general public.

- **Tier 2:** Companies can raise up to $75 million annually but must meet more detailed reporting and disclosure standards, including providing SEC-grade audited financial statements filed and reviewed by the SEC, that are similar to those required for public companies. This makes Tier 2 an ideal choice for more established businesses seeking significant capital for expansion or major projects, as the increased transparency and rigorous reporting offer investors a clearer picture of the company's financial health and reduce perceived risks. Tier 2 is what is now commonly known as REG A+ and truly is an on-ramp to public markets as a 'mini-IPO.'

For retail investors experienced at public stock investing, Tier 2 provides the benefit of reviewing audited financials and a more thorough set of disclosures, which can make the investment feel less risky. With the ability to raise more substantial funds, companies in Tier 2 are often viewed as having a more stable foundation, making it an attractive option for those seeking larger investments with greater transparency, including institutional investors with pooled funds from investors seeking opportunities that are 'near exit' ready.

Open to Accredited and Unaccredited Investors: REG A+ allows anyone to invest like REG CF. However, there are limits on how much unaccredited investors can contribute depending on their income or net worth. Based on income disclosure, the limits are set at $2000 for individual companies and $10,000 total in a year.

SEC Filing Requirements: Companies must submit a detailed offering statement to the SEC before raising funds; this includes information about the company, its financial situation, and any potential risks to investors. To be qualified under REG A Tier II (REG A+), companies must file the following with the SEC:

Form 1-A: offering statement filed with the SEC and includes detailed info about the company, securities being offered (type and terms), and the offering itself. This is similar to a prospectus for an IPO but designed for smaller companies.

Audited Financial statements are not the usual business audits; these are much more detailed and must comply with

US Generally Accepted Accounting Principles (GAAP) or International Financial Reporting Standards.

Companies must file ongoing reports, like annual and semi-annual reports, to keep investors informed. To move forward and complete their filing for public offering on NASDAQ Small Cap, the company must meet a minimum of shares outstanding (1M), bid price ($4), and number of aggregate shareholders (300).

Pros: REG A+ offers a high capital raise limit, which makes it ideal for companies looking to raise large amounts of money. It also allows accredited and unaccredited investors to participate, broadening the investor pool. The filing of detailed financials, audited by an SEC-licensed accountant, reduces risk because the company must have stellar financial records to meet this requirement and often have multiple years of operating history.

From an investor's perspective, REG A+ offers a clear advantage due to the requirement for "SEC Level" audited financials, which is the same as what companies going through the regular IPO process must submit. This means investors can review full financial disclosures, providing a transparent view of the company's financial health and operations.

The filing and compliance process is more expensive and time-consuming than other forms of crowdfunding, making it harder for startups and businesses not ready to scale to use it; therefore, companies that pass these thresholds are considered less risky and more likely to reach an exit in the near term.

Since REG A+ is most often used for companies needing capital, they can't get it from angel groups, VCs, private equity funds, or banks. They often have seed-stage investors who have owned their shares for more than 2 years. Registering for this type of capital raise provides an exit path for their early investors, who can sell their stock at the same time for the same price as the REG A+ issuer.

Cons: A company must have a budget and strategy to market and sell its offering to the general public. Although significantly less costly than a traditional IPO, qualifying can be expensive because of the legal fees and accounting fees. Industry insiders estimate that the marketing costs to promote a REG A+ offering are at least 5% of the target raise. Therefore, it is important not to take the capital offer at face value without looking at the financial records filed to ensure the issuer's cash flow is sufficient to be successful in their target raise.

INSIDE SECRET: #16

As with all types of private investment, it is important to understand the future expectations of capital needs for each company you consider. Many seed-stage startup companies plateau after their initial rounds of capital because they overestimate how quickly revenue will come in and underestimate how much revenue will be needed to support their entire operations. When a company plateaus and doesn't continue raising capital in anticipation of future needs, doesn't properly plan their investment of capital and time it takes to raise money under any of the crowdfunding provisions, your investment will languish, and you may never see an exit. This is why it is imperative to create and adhere to objective requirements and build a diverse portfolio as taught in The Compassionalist Academy.

Conclusion

Each of the four types of equity crowdfunding is suited for different kinds of businesses and fundraising needs. As an investor, whether you're looking to support a small local business, capitalize on the potential of a growing startup, or provide substantial funding to an established company, crowdfunding offers a range of options to align with your investment objectives. This flexible financing model allows you to diversify your portfolio and potentially access high-growth opportunities across various sectors and stages of development. By understanding the differences between these models, businesses can choose the one that best suits their needs, and investors can understand what to expect before putting their money into a crowdfunding campaign.

To sum up, crowdfunding represents a monumental shift in how individuals can participate in financing businesses. Whether you're interested in supporting a local restaurant or shop that is expanding, backing an innovative startup solving a problem you are passionate about, or investing in real estate projects outside of your financial reach, crowdfunding platforms offer many opportunities. Through equity, debt, and revenue-sharing models, crowdfunding offers investors diverse opportunities to grow their portfolios, and support causes they believe in, with built-in protections.

Jane decides to 'give it a go'. Jane determines to diversify by stage and industry. She invests in early-stage startups via Regulation Crowdfunding (REG CF), making smaller, high-risk investments. For larger opportunities, *she uses Reg A+ offerings, where she can invest in more established companies that look to scale and exit. Since her income is under $200,000, she's ineligible for Rule 506(c) but benefits from Reg A+ to access established company investment opportunities. As Jane builds out her initial portfolio of 10 investments, into three categories:*

- *Income-producing*

- *Innovative Startups*

- *Established Growth Stage*

She will seek diversity in the industry and among founders.

Ch. Three: Creating Your Investment Strategy

By now, you should be aware that crowdfunding offers an exciting opportunity to invest in startups, innovative products, and early-stage businesses. However, investing in private companies also carries a unique set of challenges compared to other asset classes in which you might have already invested or planned to invest. As an investor, one of the most pressing questions you will ask yourself is: What should I invest in, and how much should I commit?

Earlier, you learned that Jane had $40,000 in savings and sufficient cash flow liquidity every month to allocate $20,000 for her entrepreneur investment portfolio. She can continue to save for life's emergencies while she starts creating her portfolio of crowdfunding investments. To do that confidently, she needed to assess her overall financial well-being to ensure she didn't invest more than she could afford. From her work, Jane knows success in caring for patients requires a plan of action and processes to follow. She wants to figure out how to identify the companies doing things she cares about, and even cool solutions she wouldn't have ever thought of without hearing about it the first time. She wonders if she would have thought Facebook was a good idea if she didn't "know about Facebook." She is eager to learn how to diversify while still investing in what she knows and what she cares about.

These questions are central to any investment strategy, especially in the crowdfunding space, where opportunities can be high-risk but also have high rewards. Over the many years that I have worked with hundreds of angel investors and interviewed dozens more on my podcast, The Compassionate Capitalist Show, I learned five aspects of angel investing and its younger sibling, crowdfund investing, that you must adopt in order to be successful investing in startups and growing small businesses. You will learn about them in the next two chapters:

1. Determine how much you can afford to invest annually and repeatedly.

2. Commit to making at least 10 investments over a finite period of time. The time frame will be driven by the average amount of your individual investments.

3. Become disciplined to invest in what you know and can verify about the deal, so that you don't let emotion cloud your judgment.

4. Diversify your investments to build a portfolio that has balanced risk with rewards.

5. When you find your rhythm in making investments in entrepreneurs, the positive feelings are hard to describe in one word. Perhaps "zest". Investing with *purpose*, in your *passions*, and making a *profit* becomes a part of your life.

Although I talk about it in my book, *Inside Secrets to Angel Investing*, I realized in hindsight that all the step-by-step insights I shared in that book didn't really explain how or provide a strategy for building a portfolio. Clarity on the strategy grew as I began to advise new investors and worked to bring that book to life as a digital course. Over time, the course evolved into a comprehensive financial literacy platform on how to get started as a crowdfunding investor and develop better skills to be a successful angel investor. That platform is The Compassionalist Academy, already referenced.

In this chapter, I'll help you navigate these fundamental directives by discussing how to evaluate your wealth, liquidity, and risk tolerance to make informed and strategic decisions that align with your financial goals. Crowdfunding is often considered an investment strategy for startups with no track record. However, as you explore the different platforms and offering structures, you will realize that companies raising capital through crowdfunding and direct public offerings are quite diverse. Fundamentally, *"crowd"* simply means **the public**. Similar to the stock market, anybody can invest; the difference is that the stock is private and illiquid. Yet the 'funding' can be structured in many ways:

- Equity Purchase

- Debt Instrument

- Revenue Share Payback

Regardless of the nature of the offering, the type of crowdfunding, or the stage of the company, it is vital to understand your financial standing fully before you commit. The goal of this chapter is to help you get a clear picture of what you can afford to invest while setting the groundwork for a thoughtful, diversified portfolio.

Identifying Your Wealth and Liquidity

Before considering how much money to invest in crowdfunding, it's essential to assess your financial situation, both your wealth and liquidity. Wealth isn't just about how much cash you have in your bank account; it encompasses all your assets, including real estate, stocks, bonds, retirement savings, and other investments. When it comes to crowdfunding, it's crucial to understand the distinction between liquid and illiquid assets.

Liquid assets are those that can be easily converted into cash, such as cash savings, money market funds, and publicly traded stocks. Illiquid assets, on the other hand, such as collectibles, long-term investments like real estate or privately held ventures, are more difficult to sell quickly at their true value. Retirement accounts such as a 401k are typically illiquid without penalties for withdrawing before your eligible age milestone. However, a 'self-directed retirement account' like ROTH IRA or Self-Directed IRA can be structured to invest in alternative investments such as real estate AND private company equity.

Understanding your liquidity is critical in angel investing and crowdfunding, as these types of investments are most often illiquid, meaning you won't be able to quickly access your money if needed. Private equity investments in startups or other early-stage ventures can take years to yield a return (or to lose it all if the business doesn't succeed). Therefore, before you make any commitment, it's important to determine how much of your wealth can realistically be tied up in these long-term, illiquid investments without jeopardizing your ability to meet short-term financial obligations or handle emergencies.

Tools like the Wealth & Liquidity Calculator©, which are available in our Compassionalist Academy course material, can guide you through this process. The calculator helps you evaluate your financial assets, understand how liquid (or illiquid) your portfolio is, and determine how much you can safely allocate to crowdfunding projects.

Jane used the Wealth & Liquidity Calculator to look at the financial situation from a different perspective. She confirmed that her income was consistently more than her expenses on a monthly basis. She typically got a pay raise every other year. She had been contributing to her 401K that her employer matched, and it had grown to be worth about $300,000. She had about 10 years left on her mortgage, but her home had almost doubled in value. She had inherited a house from her parents that still had a small mortgage, but the rental income covered the payment with a little leftover to handle the maintenance and repairs. Her assets were not over a million dollars, so she would be investing as an unaccredited investor.

Jane had long had a 'side hustle' teaching a Zumba class every week. She was helping her son with his living expenses at college, but he would be graduating soon, and her daughter had a scholarship. She felt comfortable redirecting $20,000 of her savings toward crowdfunding investments because she could continue to make her regular savings allocation. Her 'Zumba money' could go toward vacations or the occasional 'big bill.' She would reassess annually.

By assessing your overall wealth, including retirement savings, property value, and investments, and then analyzing the liquid portion of your portfolio, you'll gain a clearer idea of how much capital you can allocate to crowdfunding without compromising your financial security. For instance, you might find that while your total wealth is substantial, a large chunk of it is tied up in real estate or business ventures that are difficult to liquidate quickly.

INSIDE SECRET: #18

THE DECISION TO ADOPT ANY WEALTH CREATION STRATEGY MUST BE BALANCED WITH A WEALTH PRESERVATION STRATEGY.

The Angel Profitability Blueprint

Once you have a firm understanding of your financial position, it's time to put a strategy into place. Crowdfunding offers the possibility of high returns, but these opportunities come with significant risks. That's why diversification is so critical. One of the most effective strategies for building a sustainable and profitable angel and crowdfunding portfolio is to start out with a goal of making ten investments over an intentional time frame.

Once you have identified your readily available pool of liquid funds, divide that by 10. If the outcome feels uncomfortable to start with, you can split that amount and add it to the number of investments your pool of funds will be invested in. Then the time frame, whether your goal will be 2 years or some timeframe longer than that, is based on your commitment of time to gain skills and follow the steps to build a diversified, profitable portfolio.

You need to strive to have many different investments so that you can spread the risk and increase the rewards. This approach is built on the principle of diversification; by spreading your investments across different projects and sectors, you reduce the overall risk of your portfolio. Crowdfund investment portfolios, as with angel investment portfolios, increase in value over time.

When you reach the halfway point of investing your initial 'wealth chest', you will reassess your financial situation and decide how much can be allocated every year and how many investments can be made. As you become more confident, you may decide to invest larger amounts in fewer companies while the total allocation of funds remains the same. For example, starting out, you might invest in 10 opportunities for $500 each or smaller amounts in the ones that you simply love but realize may have more risk. This will allow you to invest more in the opportunities that will produce income, $2000 if you are not yet accredited.

The Angel Profitability Blueprint is designed to strategically help you make these diversified investments. The blueprint advocates for investing in companies at different stages of growth, in various industries, and offering different structures.

1. Stages of Growth: Seed, Startup, Early, Emerging, Growth, Exit

2. Various Industries: Tech, Consumer Goods, Healthcare, BioMed, Software, AI (Artificial Intelligence), VR (Virtual Reality), Gaming, Esports, Blockchain, etc.

3. Offering Structure: Revenue Share, Debt, Convertible Note, SAFE, Equity

Fundamentally, the return on investment is achieved when the original purchase price of private equity stock is less than the sales price of the equity ownership when the company is acquired or goes public. In other words, if the share was purchased for $1 and it goes public at $10, you made 10X your investment ($9 on each share, less capital gains tax).

Greater returns on your investment are expected from startups and early-stage innovation-driven companies because the cost of the shares is lower than it will be in the future, as their business model is proven and they execute their strategy to scale.

INSIDE SECRET: #19

THE BIG RETURNS SEASONED ANGEL INVESTORS REPORT COME FROM THE BALANCE OF THEIR PORTFOLIO, WITH MOSTLY SEED AND STARTUP INVESTMENTS THAT "HIT BIG" AND MAKE UP FOR THE LOSSES. THE COMPASSIONATE CAPITALIST APPROACH IS TO CREATE A DIVERSE PORTFOLIO THAT BALANCES RISKY STARTUP INVESTING WITH PREDICTABLE INCOME-PRODUCING AND LESS RISKY LATE-STAGE INVESTING.

Although I am not a financial advisor, I have learned from my own personal experience and that of numerous seasoned angel investors over the years. I recommend balancing these high-risk investments with opportunities that are later-stage, with a proven track record and sustainable cash flow. The ROI may not be as great as that of a startup, but there will still be a healthy profit for your investment that is better than most public stock opportunities. A company going through a REG A+ offering may have a stock price of $10, but with the capital, it raises to expand its product line, grow geographically, or acquire another company's business, it may double or triple its business. That could lead to them going public at $20 or $30 a share, giving a nice double or triple your ROI.

Although private investments structured as debt have always been an aspect of private (angel) investing, they were typically one-offs, not something a group of angels participated in. I have long been an advocate of this type of investment, particularly for new angel investors. In my first book, *Inside Secrets to Angel Investing*, the story of Jack and the chapter "Making of a Compassionate Capitalist," and his first investment was a bridge note. I included a section, "When an Investor is a Bank," in the book as well. That book is still available on Amazon and is included in *The Compassionalist Academy* – **Intro to Angel & Crowdfund Investing** training.

As Jane starts building her portfolio, she starts with investments that would produce a short-term gain and an income stream. Getting even a small return early on gave her confidence, and she felt comfortable taking time to find startup equity investment opportunities that she was passionate about and could fully review. She anticipated higher long-term gains from her startup investments, while the growth stage companies raising capital could lead to a SmallCap IPO and a nearer-term exit from those investments.

A diverse portfolio must also include investing across different sectors. Using *The Wealth & Liquidity Calculator*, you will determine which sectors you are knowledgeable about and, therefore, can look for opportunities in those different industries and use cases. You will want to look for opportunities in what would be considered more stable sectors, such as healthcare, energy, or consumer goods. For example, while you might choose to invest in five tech startups, you should also consider investments in industries that are more recession-resistant, such as renewable energy, food production, or infrastructure. By doing so, you help protect your portfolio from downturns in any one sector, thereby increasing the likelihood of success across the board.

The Compassionalist Academy guides you on how to vet projects, understand the founder's track record, assess the company's financial projections, and evaluate the crowdfunding platform itself. By following these steps, you can make informed decisions that will help you build a strong, diversified portfolio that maximizes returns and minimizes unnecessary risk.

Understandably, Jane was nervous about investing in 'businesses' because she didn't think of herself as being business-savvy. She hadn't owned or operated a business, so she didn't have first-hand experience. She hadn't studied any more business than the 'business management' course she took in college. With some guidance, she learned what to look for as red flags and how to apply her earned experience from working in different jobs, where she had mentally noted over the years what worked and didn't work that helped or hindered those companies to succeed. As Jane evaluated and compared different opportunities, she was able to gain confidence to

invest in companies that she liked and had reasonable expectations of success.

You start first with a specific intent to build a portfolio of 10 companies, but patience is a virtue when it comes to managing your risk. The tool, *The Wealth & Liquidity Calculator,* helps you calculate a risk score as you look at deals and run them through your filter based on the type of offer, stage, and industry. It helps to prevent the #1 reason for a bad investment – investing on emotion rather than objective criteria.

INSIDE SECRET: #20

BUILDING YOUR PORTFOLIO IS NOT A WALK IN THE PARK. IT WILL TAKE A COMMITMENT OF TIME AND MONEY. IT WILL BE WORTH IT WHEN YOU FIND OPPORTUNITIES THAT ARE REWARDING ON TWO LEVELS:

PASSION AND PROFIT

Find What You Know and Love

One of the unique benefits of crowdfunding investment is the opportunity to support projects that align with your personal interests, passions, and expertise. When you invest in areas where you already have knowledge or deep interest, you not only improve your ability to evaluate the company's potential, but you also increase the chances that you'll stay engaged with the project long-term.

Jane had experience in healthcare as a career, and she knew where there were opportunities for innovation in that industry. Jane was a mother and a grandmother-to-be, so she felt that she had a good understanding of consumer products for that target market. Jane was also an outdoor enthusiast and loved water sports. As she considered her vocational experience, hobbies, and other lived experiences, she realized she knew a lot more than she gave herself credit for. She often thought, "This could be better if they did x or y or z."

Innovation can come from new software systems or even new types of devices or technologies that make it easier to care for patients in recovery. Sometimes, our experiences in an industry come from life experiences we have lived through the care of our friends and family in short-term or long-term care scenarios. We can recognize a solution to a problem from our life experience and vocational/educational training.

One of the reasons I was so excited was that it became legal for companies to raise capital from the public, and the public could invest before the stock was 'retail,' I truly believed it would (and will continue to) bring more and more capital into the market to support really terrific companies solving real problems in profound ways. As rich as the High Net Worth (HNW) investors are, they don't ALL invest in private companies.

There are a lot more non-accredited investors than there are accredited. By writing my first book, bringing that to life with *The Compassionalist Academy,* and now this follow-on book and more entry-level training, I was excited to unlock the potential for more worthy companies to get access to capital, more problems to be solved, more fun and joy to be created, and more prosperity for all. Hence, the more invested you are in the project's success, both financially and emotionally, the more likely you are to monitor its progress, make informed decisions, and provide valuable feedback.

For example, if you have a background in sustainable energy, you may find investing in a solar panel startup not only exciting but also something you can evaluate effectively. Your understanding of the market and technology might give you insights others may lack, which could make you a more effective investor. As you follow the investment over time, you may invest more or find you can contribute in other ways as an advisor or refer them to business and alliance opportunities that contribute to their success beyond investment capital and help steer the project toward success. Further, as an industry, it isn't considered disruptive, and there are opportunities in that sector that are both early-stage tech and established profitable implementations and infrastructure companies.

On the flip side, investing in a sector you're unfamiliar with simply because it is 'hot' and there is a lot of buzz, like AI, a revolutionary cancer treatment, or a new social media platform, can lead to poor decision-making. You might fail to see red flags, lose your money, and become disillusioned as time goes on. Your passion for the solution is a catalyst, and your patience in evaluating the fundamentals of the business drives better results.

In the course, we discuss in detail how to identify the industries that excite you and where your skills and experience can add value in evaluating the true merits of going from an idea to a working solution in the market.

Navigating Uncertainty

Risk is an inherent part of investing. History has proven the stock market can tank, the real estate market can pop and flatten, and crypto probably has the most uncertainty. In crowdfunding, as with angel investing, the "uncertainty" isn't inherent in the act of investing in a private company. The risk and uncertainty are heightened by the nature of the majority of investment opportunities. Traditionally, angel investors have usually focused on startups and early-stage companies because of the huge upside potential, factoring in the increased risk at that stage of a company's lifecycle. Furthermore, they invest because:

1. They desire to create an impact on their investments by helping entrepreneurs they admire and believe in, solving problems they care about.

2. The thrill of knowing that your investment is at the lowest price it should ever be contributes to maximizing the potential return over any other type of investment.

Most crowdfunding investing is similar to angel investing. The majority of REG CF projects are startups or early-stage ventures, meaning they are untested in the market and can face significant operational and financial challenges. Understanding how to assess and manage risk is, therefore, essential to being a successful crowdfunding investor.

Remember that the overall category of crowdfunding includes the following types: REG CF, REG A+, REG D 506c, and Intrastate Exemption. Each is suited for different companies at different stages with different funding needs. They are only similar because they raise money from the crowd. "Direct Public Offerings"

INSIDE SECRET: #21

*THERE IS LESS 'HEARD ON THE STREET'
STOCK TIPS AND PUBLIC ANALYSIS
SURROUNDING PRIVATE COMPANIES THAN
FOR PUBLIC COMPANIES OR BIG COMPANIES
'GOING PUBLIC'. THEREFORE, IT IS
IMPORTANT TO COMMIT TO CONDUCTING
DUE DILIGENCE AND A CAREFUL
EVALUATION OF EACH INVESTMENT.*

Just because a crowdfunding platform lists an issuer, and that company presents a compelling and seemingly lucrative opportunity, you should never invest without carefully researching the company, its leadership team, its market, and its financial health. Without proper research, you might find yourself investing in a project that lacks a clear path to profitability or is valued so high the ROI on the stock will be a challenge, or the terms of the investment may make it difficult to get a good return on investment.

It was hard for Jane to resist some of the first investments that she saw. Their videos were so compelling, and the opportunity seemed reasonable. By following the principles behind the Angel Profitability Blueprint, Jane found her folding kayak company because she saw another company with something similar in a paddleboard. She started looking up portable watercraft on the different sites and joined the platforms to scout and watch deals. She subscribed to the websites of the companies she was watching to see how they did marketing outreach and customer cultivation. As she compared and watched, she ended up having three different companies solving the problem in different ways. She was able to pick one that best met her individual needs for structure, stage, and value.

Factoring in the stage of the business or progress the company has made during its time in business, as you consider investing in that company, is important as part of the risk/reward and diversification strategy. Startup companies often lack a proven track record, making them high-risk investments. It is a reality that startup companies struggle to generate revenue. Without revenue or investment capital to bridge the gap to pay for the products and services they need to attract customers and generate revenue, they may fail to attract and sustain operations until they are cash flow positive. This isn't always a reflection on the value of the business or their solution; it is simply hard to build a large, sustainable business from 0 to $$$. When the company succeeds, the returns on your investment can be substantial.

Early-stage companies are usually 'in revenue' and may even be making a profit. They need capital to continue growing revenue, expanding operations, and bringing out new features and products. Early-stage companies work toward sustained profit. More established businesses, in the growth stage or late stage, typically offer a lower level of risk, but they also come with lower growth potential.

The key here is to decide how much risk you are willing to take and to understand what stage the company is in. If you're comfortable with high risk and potential high returns, startup and early-stage investments might appeal to you. However, if you prefer stability, investing in companies with a proven track record might be a better choice.

Industry risk is also a major consideration. For instance, the technology sector is fast-moving and highly competitive. A promising tech startup may have strong growth potential, but it could also face rapid obsolescence or intense competition. Biotech often has a great deal of regulations it must pass before it can be commercialized, which adds to the risk.

By contrast, a company in a more established industry, like transportation, manufacturing, or consumer goods, may be more stable but less likely to deliver huge returns because its cost to create revenue is higher and occurs with every sale. Understanding the industry's dynamics and the broader market forces affecting it can help you assess the potential for success.

Finally, macroeconomic factors such as interest rates, inflation, and government policy can also play a role in a crowdfund investment's success or failure. As an investor, you need to keep a finger on the pulse of these broader trends and assess how they might impact the companies you invest in.

Types of Investment Structures

Debt

Crowdfunding investments, like angel investments, come with various forms of debt structures.

1. Tied to equity that converts into equity.

2. Tied to future expectations of performance.

3. Tied to future expected contracts or venture funding.

Debt that is tied to equity is called *convertible notes* or *SAFE (Simple Agreement for Future Equity) notes*. These financial instruments allow you to provide funding to early-stage companies with the promise of future equity. They are used when the company is a startup or at a very early stage, and it is too soon to calculate its valuation and, therefore, the cost of the shares. When a company then raises its first 'institutional round' like an angel investor round, sometimes referred to as Series A, the value is established, and the convertible notes and SAFE notes are converted into that round and added to the total value of that round. The investors that hold those notes now own equity valued at the equity plus the discount or accumulated interest.

A convertible note is a form of short-term debt that converts into equity when the company raises its next round of funding. This type of investment typically includes accumulated interest that is tied to the value of the original investment, as well as additional perks such as a discount or 'coupon' on shares that they may convert in future rounds of funding. A feature available in some convertible notes is the option not to convert into equity; rather, the investor opts to be paid back the investment plus the interest.

A SAFE note is similar but doesn't carry the same debt obligation. It's an agreement that gives investors the right to convert their investment into equity during the company's next funding round, often at a discounted price. SAFE notes differ from convertible notes in that they put a cap on the value to reduce the chance of diluting the value of the needed seed capital because the company's next round is at a very high valuation.

Both convertible and SAFE notes allow investors to take part in the company's future growth without immediately taking equity ownership at a specific price. However, these types of debt-structured investments can be as risky as straight equity since there's no guarantee of returns or an immediate exit strategy.

Debt based on Future Revenue

A debt offer that is tied to future expectations of performance is typically made because an established business needs money than it can get from the bank and an alternative finance firm. They may offer up a private investment offer to their business community or their customers (*Investomers* as Sherwood Neiss coined in his best-selling book: **Investomers: How Customers-Turned-Investors are Shaping the Future of Early-Stage Finance**) to become investors. The business owner may offer collateral as part of the contract to be paid back when they are paid, or out of the revenue that will come from the expansion.

For example, a business needs to match its SBA-backed bank loan to update its facility or expand to an additional location. The loan is offered, and the company can prove that they have current cash flow plus their future increased profit from the use of the loan, which will grow their profit, and therefore, they have a strong likelihood of being able to pay their SBA loan back as well as pay their 'investors'.

Sometimes businesses are in a type of industry that may not be one that is considered favorably by traditional bank lending. Banks historically won't back a restaurant but will back a doctor's office. Even then, I have seen non-traditional medicine businesses struggle to get bank financing but be very successful in raising community-based and affinity capital from investors. "Main Street" small businesses often struggle to get bank loans to pay for soft dollar costs like marketing, employee training, needed business services, and raw materials for manufacturing, which are necessary to grow revenue.

Fortunately, the advent of crowdfunding created opportunities for REG CF platforms like Honeycomb and SMBX to offer a way for businesses to apply, qualify, and then raise capital by offering a fixed-term loan opportunity to their customers, their community, and then other investors that join those platforms looking for investments with predictable returns- not large, but predictable.

As Jane was looking to fill her portfolio with opportunities that would provide an 'income' from her investment, she was delighted to find that she could find businesses offering products she was familiar with and wanted to support their expansion. She was able to invest $1000 into a debt offer of $100,000 at 12%, paid back over 24 months. This meant she received a monthly payment of about $51, a total payback of $1240, netting $240.

Getting a return from a debt instrument will not be a big multiple, but the opportunity (and risk) of a multiple on an equity investment is offset by the predictable income earned that is **more than what a savings account or CD note would earn** *and more predictable than a stock market or crypto investment.*

Bridge Note

A Bridge Note is typically offered when the company commits to a significant investment or contract opportunity in the near term that will be the collateral. The bridge note is paid off when the company receives the investment or when the payment is received on the contract. Like any loan, a bridge note earns interest for the time of the loan, and that accumulated interest is included in the payout.

Bridge notes usually garner a higher interest rate than other loans because of their short term and critical timing to 'bridge' to the event that will keep the company growing. Depending on the circumstances, the investor may be able to negotiate a small equity position to retain after the payback. Bridge notes are not common in crowdfunding.

In *Inside Secrets to Angel Investing*, I tell the story of *Jack*. As shared previously, I use his story as an example of 'the making of a compassionate capitalist.' *Jack* was brand new to angel investing. I advised him to get started with a bridge note for the very same reasons I advise now. There was an exciting company with revolutionary technology that could rapidly scan people, containers, and anything for security in ports and airports. It could detect the difference between a bottle of liquid, such as water or nitroglycerin, or a bag of powder, such as sugar or cocaine, simply by scanning the container. Imagine not having to dump your water out at airport security. They had a commitment for a large venture capital round and needed money to make payroll and pay vendors until the VC round closed. *Jack* provided bridge finance of $75,000. He received back about $100,000, his initial investment plus accumulated interest and fees, and gained confidence in the process. He went on to invest that profit in another company for equity that produced big returns.

I am delighted to report that the company, which *Jack* helped bridge the gap with his short-term loan, issued their IPO in 2025, breaking a record on their first day of trading. They were a struggling start-up with amazing tech, but with that small (compared to the MILLIONS the company raised over 20 years), very critical point of financing, that company went on to develop additional technology that scans and eradicates pests and microbes on produce before it is sold to the public. I don't know how much *Jack* ended up making on the deal, but it was good in two ways – financially and emotionally.

INSIDE SECRET: #22

IN THE FIRST CHAPTER, I SHARED THE REASONS WHY INVESTORS TAKE RISKS ON PRIVATE EQUITY INVESTMENTS GO WAY BEYOND THE ROI AND CAPITAL GAINED BACK. IT IS THE INNOVATION THAT THEIR AND YOUR MONEY CAN BRING TO MARKET. IT IS THE IMPACT YOUR MONEY CAN HAVE ON A COMPANY THAT SCALES TO CREATE MANY JOBS. IT IS THOSE 6 HIERARCHY OF HUMAN NEEDS THAT ANGEL CROWDFUNDING FILLS THAT SOMETIMES IS MORE REWARDING THAN THE EXTRA MONEY IN THE BANK.

Revenue Share Financing

Revenue-sharing agreements are becoming an increasingly popular option for crowdfunding investors. In a revenue share arrangement, instead of receiving equity, you receive a percentage of the company's revenue until a certain percentage of the money is paid back. This structure provides a more predictable stream of income, as you are entitled to a share of the company's profits. A reasonable offer is to begin paying a percentage of the revenue after the company reaches a milestone in profit or cash flow that is established in the terms of the offer. This can be appealing if you're looking for more immediate returns rather than waiting for the company to scale.

If you have ever watched Shark Tank, then you likely know "*Mr. Wonderful*" Kevin O'Leary, who frequently asks for a percentage of the revenue. In his case, he often also makes a large enough investment that he gets equity along with a share of the revenue. Kevin O'Leary invested in StartEngine, sending vibrations through the industry that crowdfunding was a viable way for startups to grow and stage companies to raise capital through Direct Public Offerings.

The key difference between revenue share offerings and pure equity is that revenue sharing doesn't come with ownership of the company. You're not entitled to voting rights or a share of the company's equity unless specified in the agreement. Once the agreed payout is met, typically 3x the investment, but as much as 5x the investment, the founder's commitment is done. The company retains its equity, and the investor has a good return on investment. By taking a percentage of the revenue rather than equity, in this example, the investors receives income throughout the life of that payout commitment and do not have to wait until a milestone value is reached and an exit event occurs to see a return on their investment

As Jane looked to fill her portfolio according to the strategy she learned using the Angel Profitability Blueprint, she found a company she was familiar with because she had bought their product when her daughter was having her baby. She saw they were bringing out a line of products for toddlers. She trusted their quality. She

could look at their past financial performance from their financial statements. She could reasonably assess that adding this additional product line would grow their revenue, and she looked forward to receiving a quarterly payout as the company grew with the money she and others in the crowd invested.

INSIDE SECRET: #23

REVENUE SHARE TERMS ARE UNIQUE TO EACH DEAL AND WILL VARY BASED ON MANY FACTORS:
PURPOSE OF THE MONEY;
IMPACT ON REVENUE GROWTH;
STRUCTURE OF THE PAYOUT AS A PERCENTAGE OF OVERALL REVENUE OR DIRECTLY TIED TO THAT NEW PRODUCT OR LOCATION;
THE DURATION OF THE PAYOUT IS TYPICALLY UNTIL SOME MULTIPLE OF THE INITIAL INVESTMENT IS REACHED.

In conclusion, crowdfunding offers exciting opportunities for high returns; however, it naturally comes with risks. To succeed, it's crucial to evaluate your financial position, liquidity, and risk tolerance before committing. Investing in areas where you have passion and expertise can also improve your chances of success. Whether you choose equity-based investments or revenue sharing, aligning your investments with your goals and risk profile will help ensure a more strategic and rewarding approach to crowdfunding.

Ch. Four: Building a Diverse Portfolio

Congratulations! You have succeeded in the first crucial steps on your journey to become a successful investor in entrepreneurs – You are over halfway through this book! Hopefully, you've started getting comfortable with the basics, pinpointing what drives you and what you are interested in, and figuring out how much you have to invest this year, and each year after that. Maybe you have even mapped out your strategy to build your portfolio and started to set up accounts to find the opportunities. That would be grand. If not, no worries. Keep going and remember there is training and hands-on guidance available for you when you want it.

Chapter Four takes all the insights you have gained thus far a step further, focusing on the deliberate process of identifying opportunities that align with your financial goals and personal values while also developing a structured plan to guide your decisions. This chapter will walk you through each step, using Jane's experience as a detailed example, and weave in every point we've discussed. Let's dive into the process.

Figuring It Out: Finding Deals - Jane's Journey

You can start your hunt for the deals that excite you when you are equipped with the following key factors:

1. What is your total capital available to invest, and is your cash on hand or allocated within your retirement account?
2. Are you limited to the max of $2000 in any one deal, or $10,000 a year total based on current income and net worth?
3. What industries or sectors do you feel best equipped to evaluate?
4. What problems/opportunities have you thought of that you wish someone would invent, or open that business?
5. Are you confident in your understanding of basic business principles regarding profit/loss calculations, business lifecycle, and operational issues to evaluate the viability of an opportunity?
6. Are you committed to making at least 10 investments with your available capital?

INSIDE SECRET: #24

IDEALLY, THE PROSPECT OF CREATING WEALTH BY INVESTING IN INNOVATION YOU WANT TO SEE BROUGHT INTO THE WORLD AND HELPING LOCAL BUSINESSES IN YOUR COMMUNITY THRIVE IS SUFFICIENT MOTIVATION FOR YOU TO BECOME A 'HABITUAL CROWDFUND INVESTOR.'

To master any new skill or create a new positive habit takes a commitment of time and focus to learn and master. To be physically fit may take adopting a new exercise routine or trying a new sport. Starting a new job often takes time and commitment to get acclimated to the new processes and policies. Learning and mastering investing in entrepreneurs as an asset class also requires a commitment of time and focus, and the emotional and financial rewards will be worth it.

Jane has $20,000 earmarked for crowdfunding investments, and she's approaching this with intention. Building on the premise of the Angel Profitability Blueprint explained in Chapter Three, she has already secured two income-generating investments: a stake in a local business she trusts and is excited to see them open up another location closer to her home, and a real estate crowdfunding venture that provides a share of rental income on a beautiful 'Live, Work, Play' multiuse complex on the river in her home town.

These are solid starting points, but Jane's sights are set higher. She wants her investment money to do more than just grow; she wants it to address issues she cares deeply about.

As Jane worked through her earned and learned experience, she had an 'aha' moment. Her motivation crystallized as she reflected on a personal experience the previous year when her daughter had a baby. Jane noticed how her daughter struggled with inefficient baby products, like a stroller that was cumbersome and ill-suited to her busy life. This observation led Jane to investigate companies that are innovating in this space.

Jane reflected on the evolution of baby gear: in the past, car seats and strollers were separate, bulky items; then came integrated designs; and now, she discovered firms pushing boundaries further, like a stroller that doubles as a car seat and a highchair. She started a digital journal to jot down ideas to look into and started using the AI bot on her phone to help her identify what companies might be working on innovations in the baby & childcare products market.

Considering this logical progression fascinated her and sparked an idea: what other everyday challenges could be solved through smart investments? Her focus soon shifted to healthcare, fueled by real-world frustrations she'd encountered. At her workplace, colleagues frequently mentioned persistent problems: germs spreading between patients due to poor sanitation practices, and medication errors caused by miscommunication during shift changes because staff jotted notes down on paper and therefore required data entry to sync with digital updates in the Patient Management System.

These weren't hypothetical issues; they were inefficiencies Jane had seen disrupt lives, including those of people she cared about. She began to wonder if she could support companies tackling these exact problems, merging her investment goals with a sense of purpose. For example, she recalled her daughter's postpartum experience, where the lack of innovative maternal care products stood out. This is tied to broader healthcare concerns, such as how hospitals struggled with germ transmission or ensuring that the right patient got the right treatment at the right time. Jane realized that finding deals wasn't just about profit; it was about backing solutions to problems she'd witnessed firsthand. This realization became her north star as she embarked on her search.

INSIDE SECRET #25

CROWDFUNDING METHODOLOGY CAN BE CONFUSING BECAUSE ALTHOUGH REG CF PLATFORMS ARE TYPICALLY USED BY STARTUPS TO RAISE MONEY, YOU WILL ALSO FIND COMPANIES THAT HAVE RAISED SUBSTANTIAL MONEY FROM ANGELS AND VCS, RAISING ADDITIONAL CAPITAL. WHEN THIS HAPPENS, IT IS USUALLY TO GROW THEIR BRAND AWARENESS, INCREASE THE NUMBER OF SHAREHOLDERS, AND RAISE WORKING CAPITAL SO THEY CAN BE IN A BETTER POSITION TO GO PUBLIC, EVEN AS A STEPPINGSTONE TO A REG A+ TO SCALE AND EXIT ON THE PUBLIC EXCHANGES.

Getting started was simple; Jane visited the platforms we've mentioned before, Wefunder, StartEngine, and

Republic, created accounts, entered basic personal details, linked a bank account, and specified her interest areas, like healthcare and sustainable innovation.

This setup process mirrors opening an online account for any service, but with a twist: once registered, these platforms use your preferences to send tailored deal suggestions. It's a practical way to filter the vast number of opportunities into a manageable stream.

Jane didn't limit herself to the major players, though. She learned there were niche platforms catering to specific sectors, like biomedicine, cancer research, or even entertainment. Using search engines like Google and Yahoo (she deliberately avoided over-relying on one tool), she explored phrases such as "healthcare crowdfunding platforms," "blockchain startups raising capital," and "IoT healthcare solutions." She searched and uncovered companies running their own Reg A+ campaigns on private portals, bypassing traditional platforms.

This expanded Jane's horizons (and prospects), showing her that opportunities existed beyond the obvious venues. She also considered how companies might not always use REG CF or Reg A+. She hadn't thought of it before, but she remembered getting memos about clinical trials being conducted in the 'teaching hospital' wing of her hospital. Early-stage firms might conduct beta tests, like a healthcare startup trialing a new system in a local hospital, while raising capital independently. Jane made a mental note to check company websites for "investors" tabs, where such opportunities might be listed.

Building a Wishlist: Searching by Industry and Tracking Progress

Getting started in crowdfund investing can be overwhelming. A company selling products to the public is not much different than selling its stock to an investor. With customers, they compete with companies that solve a similar problem or fulfill a common need of their customers. A company selling its stock to investors must compete with other companies raising capital. There are not enough investors or capital for all the companies raising capital (which is why you and everyone else reading this book and getting educated are so important to fund innovation, create jobs, and keep the economy humming). Every company is competing to be chosen, almost like a beauty contest. They create pitches and videos, trying to be the prettiest and most engaging. They tout benefits like they are the only ones solving this problem and the ones that will offer the most return on your investment.

Without having a game plan to work from, you can be paralyzed with uncertainty on where to start and how to discern *this* over *that*. That is why my unique approach is to start with income-producing investments so you can give yourself the grace to find the gems that have the most potential to succeed. It also helps you to avoid the inevitable anxiety of new investors – "when will I get my money back, get that return on investment?" – because it is rarely as soon as you want, and sometimes double the time of what you expected. This is a fundamental principle of the Angel Profitability Blueprint. Whether you use a digital diary, notebook, or a spreadsheet to jot ideas down, list deals to watch, or score a company under consideration, it doesn't matter. Work within your style in organizing your thoughts and action items. What is important is to establish the guardrails of your journey in order to avoid the risk of an emotional investment.

INSIDE SECRETS: #26

EVERY ENTREPRENEUR THINKS THEIR DEAL IS THE BEST. IT IS PART OF THEIR DNA AND PART OF THEIR JOB AS FOUNDER AND VISIONARY. REALIZING THEY ARE 'SELLING YOU' IS IMPORTANT TO UNDERSTAND, BECAUSE UNLIKE A PRODUCT THAT ENDS UP NOT BEING AS GREAT AS YOU EXPECTED, YOU CAN'T RETURN IT. IT IS IMPORTANT TO BE METHODICAL IN YOUR ACCUMULATION OF OPPORTUNITIES SO AS NOT TO BECOME OVERWHELMED INTO INACTION, SCREENING THEM TO NARROW YOUR OPTIONS TO PRESERVE YOUR TIME, THEN COMMITTING TO SPENDING SUFFICIENT TIME ON DUE DILIGENCE TO BE AS AWARE AS POSSIBLE ABOUT THE RISKS.

With her accounts active, Jane began her hunt. She approached the hunt systematically, treating it like compiling a wish list, akin to saving items on Amazon for later review. On each platform, she searched by industry, starting with "healthcare innovation." Results included companies developing wearable devices to monitor patient vitals in real-time, others using blockchain to secure medical records against breaches, and some blending IoT with air purification to reduce germ transmission.

When a company piqued her interest, she marked it, often with a heart icon or a "watch" button, similar to favoriting a post online, adding it to her list of prospects. Jane didn't stop at one platform; she cross-checked her findings across multiple sites, looking for similar solutions executed differently, and jotting the most compelling into her digital notepad. For instance, if she found a firm using IoT to track patient data, she'd search for competitors employing AI-driven diagnostics or novel filtration systems to address the same germ-transmission problem. This comparative approach helped her understand the landscape and identify standout players.

To stay informed, she set up news alerts using Google News and other services for terms like "healthcare blockchain," "patient data startups," and "IoT medical devices." Setting alerts keeps her up to date with all the breaking news, such as a company making headlines or an industry trend gaining traction. She also monitored social media chatter and tapped into workplace conversations, like asking her IT colleague about tech trends in hospitals, to broaden her perspective.

Jane knew better than to jump in blindly. When a company's mission to reduce shift-change errors resonated with her, she dug deeper. She visited their websites, looking for investor sections detailing funding rounds or timelines. She reviewed platform disclosures, such as financial statements or campaign Q&As. If information was sparse, she posted questions directly: "How do you plan to scale this technology?" "What's your strategy for FDA approval?" or "How do you ensure HIPAA compliance?" The responses either bolstered her confidence or flagged concerns, refining her wish list over time.

She loved her sense of expectation for what was to come, the zest of the hunt, and the feeling of influence and impact she could have with her dollars. Her family and friends even started noticing the change. Her son and her best friend decided to take the step forward too and began learning the steps to become confident and competent investing as crowdfund/angel investors.

Investing Can be Fun

If you recall from Chapter 1, Angel Investing satisfies the six hierarchy of human needs:

1. Certainty: knowing your money will have an impact on solving problems you care about and supporting businesses you care about.

2. Uncertainty: not knowing the exact outcome or level of success, for the company that you own a piece of with your investment.

3. Significance: By investing in a business that can meaningfully contribute to technological advancements that improve our lives or simply contribute to the fabric of a local economy, angel investors feel they are investing in something meaningful.

4. Connection: The popular reference to the motivation for a seed stage investment, "investing in the jockey or the horse," became vogue because angel investors often make their final decision on one deal over another because they feel a connection to the founder.

5. Growth: the very nature of the business lifecycle is growth…growth from an idea at the seed stage, through startup and emerging growth, to maturity. Investing in a company to plant those seeds and watch them grow is quite rewarding.

6. Contribution: Investing in entrepreneurs and the companies they are striving to build directly contributes to job creation and the economy, more so than any other type of investment.

When you can feel good about creating wealth with your investments, that is a whole lot of fun.

As Jane opened her eyes to the vast number of entrepreneurs working hard to solve the problems she cared about, something happened. She would stream movies and TV shows and scroll through social media videos most nights. Once she had completed the Intro course and started hunting, she found it exciting. Sometimes she listened to her records or favorite playlist while she researched innovation or imagined solutions to problems, she was curious about, instead of streaming a show. Watching funny cat videos or some guy in a car venting about something wasn't nearly as engaging as watching the entrepreneur pitch videos on the crowdfunding platforms.

Researching Solutions and Companies

"Best Practice" for getting started in an intentional and methodical manner is to focus on the problem you want to solve, then find a company you like that is working on it. Learn to love that company by exploring its competitors and all the alternative approaches used by other companies. Your due diligence on a 'solution' will come in stages:

1. Initial screening of what the company touts.

2. Exploring competition and alternatives in the market.

3. Deeper dive to validate their strategy, numbers, milestones, and claims.

4. Understanding the capital structure and valuation is necessary to calculate a roadmap to an exit and return on investment.

Jane built an informal network of trusted advisors she could call or text about an article she read. If something came up about the due diligence or deal terms that she didn't understand, she could return to the Compassionalist Academy to review or send a message to the support team.

Jane's curiosity about healthcare solutions led her to technologies like IoT (Internet of Things) and Blockchain. Initially, these terms were foreign to her. It was easy to use her AI chat tool to ask questions about technology and trends. Since her tech-savvy son was supportive in her quest, she also leaned on him for his insights and had some great conversations over Sunday dinner about the impact of blockchain on patient record management.

IoT, she discovered, involves interconnected devices sharing data, like a hospital sensor alerting staff to a patient's change in condition or passively capturing vitals for analysis. Blockchain, often pigeonholed as cryptocurrency, proved far more versatile: it's a secure ledger for tracking data, ensuring, say, that a patient's medication history isn't altered or lost. One company caught her eye: it used IoT and blockchain to overhaul patient care logistics. Nurses could scan a QR code tied to a patient's file, updating it instantly across a secure network, no longer relying on paper notes that got misplaced or outdated during shift changes. The system could even flag inconsistencies, like a mismatch between a paper record and the digital version, ensuring accuracy. Jane saw its potential to solve problems she'd observed, like germ transmission from sloppy handoffs or medication errors due to poor communication.

Jane decided to do some research and investigate further, so she checked the team's credentials. Do they have healthcare veterans or tech experts? She reviewed financials on the platform, assessing whether they were burning cash too quickly or had a sustainable runway. She then consulted her IT colleague, who explained how blockchain's security aligns with HIPAA requirements, preventing data breaches that could expose patient diagnoses online. He also noted IoT's role in modern hospitals, like voice-activated systems transmitting a doctor's orders directly to a lab, bypassing handwritten notes prone to errors.

Jane's research extended beyond this company; she explored how blockchain prevents broader issues, like surgical mistakes, from operating on the wrong patient due to data mix-ups. She learned it's used in supply chains to verify product authenticity (e.g., ensuring imported goods aren't counterfeits) and in disaster recovery, like digitizing records to prevent a repeat of the great loss experienced after hurricanes and floods like with Katrina in Louisiana or destructive fires that seem to be an annual event in the west, where paper files and records vanish.

Blockchain's Non-Fungible Token (NFT) applications intrigued her, and collectors used it to prove ownership of valuables destroyed in such events, a concept she found clever, if unrelated to her focus. Her goal was clear: find a healthcare solution addressing germ transmission, medication accuracy, or record-keeping inefficiencies. She wanted something leveraging IoT for passive data capture, like a device tracking patient interactions, and blockchain for security, ensuring data moved seamlessly, securely, and safely through a care cycle. Her due diligence confirmed this company's promise, but she kept searching for competitors to compare.

Finding Opportunities Across Platforms

As you crystallize your priorities for the type of company, industry, and stage, as well as the problem being solved, it is important to set yourself up for success by researching and exploring all the options. It is easier than ever because of intelligent search engines, subscriptions to news and announcements, and Artificial Intelligence (AI) tools.

Historically, angel investors have been limited to the deals approved to present by their network or club. They could belong to many groups and national networks, attend venture forums, and join online pitch events to expand their access to deals and general awareness of the types of opportunities available to invest in. Fundamentally, the reason is the nature of private vs public offerings.

Jane's hunt wasn't confined to a single platform. There was no cost to join, so she subscribed to several mainstream and niche platforms. She scoured the big ones, Wefunder, StartEngine, and Republic, for healthcare deals. She reviewed the offerings on niche platforms focused on biomedicine and health-tech, such as Experiment.com and MedStartr.

Jane used her friendly AI tools to ask questions and returned to search engines to search terms like "healthcare startups raising capital" and "blockchain patient records," uncovering companies not yet on major portals. Some ran private campaigns, like those powered with tools offered by DealMaker and Koreconx, mirroring how established brands build their own funding channels. She also looked locally and professionally.

At work, she asked her IT colleague and an administrator about solutions their hospital was testing, perhaps a beta program from a startup raising capital. She visited company websites, clicking the "Investors" tabs to see if they offered REG CF or Reg A+ opportunities. If a firm was solving a problem she cared about, like shift-change chaos, she checked for competitors addressing it differently, ensuring she had a full picture before committing.

Time would fly by as Jane discovered so much about innovation happening in healthcare and health tech. She would bookmark articles and websites to return to in the future and document her discoveries and her progress in her digital diary. People at work even started asking what was up because she seemed to have a new zest in her step.

Structuring the Investment Portfolio

I developed the "Angel Profitability Blueprint" as a strategy, a road map to help novice angel investors and crowdfund investors start right. Starting right means creating a clear expectation that the odds of success in creating wealth through investing in entrepreneurs grow with more investments. It's rooted in venture capital logic: pros target a 5x return per deal, but outcomes vary. In a typical 10-deal portfolio, three might fail due to market shifts, mismanagement, or external shocks like a pandemic draining reserves. Three might yield modest gains (25%), three could return 3-5x, and one might explode (10x or more).

Crowdfunding, however, is rewriting this script. In 2025, the first company to go IPO after it started raising capital under REG CF. Beta Bionics raised $1 million in seed-stage capital on Wefunder in 2016 and went public with a $1B market cap. With stock splits and restructuring along the way, it is hard to tell if those early investors got the face value return of 100x. It shows that the crowdfunding market is maturing and validates the potential for outsized wins in less than a decade.

With a robust wish list, Jane needed a plan. She appreciated the investment strategy offered through the Angel Profitability Blueprint. This framework helped her allocate her $20,000 across at least 10 investments, balancing risk and reward based on her tolerance and passions. Jane's blueprint hinges on her risk profile, shaped by her risk tolerance and what she's passionate about.

Jane decides to put her 20,000 to work in 3 buckets to create a balance of low risk, lower expected returns with higher risk market makers that have potential for huge payback.

1. *Income-producing and leveraged fixed-term loans.*

2. *Late stage with expectations of exits within 3 years.*

3. *Innovation that required patience and potentially multiple rounds of capital to achieve its full potential.*

Here's how it plays out depending on whether Jane is more conservative or aggressive in her risk vs reward investment strategy.

The Sliding Scale of Risk vs Reward

There are three categories used to describe an investor's risk profile: Risk Averse, Moderate Risk, and Risk Tolerant.

The allocation might look like this:

	Income Producing	De-Risked	Innovation
Risk Averse	50%	40%	10%
Moderate	40%	30%	30%
Risk Tolerant	25%	25%	50%

Their labels are pretty much self-explanatory, so let's look at how Jane would invest based on each category.

Risk Averse

Jane prefers safety, so she allocates more of her $20,000 into less risky and more predictable structured offerings. She invests $10,000 in income-producing deals, such as the real estate mixed-use project in her hometown and a fixed-term loan to a local business, for steady cash flow.

She decides to use $9,000 for investment in stable companies with $5-10 million in revenue, raising funds to scale. For example, she found an HVAC (Heating and Air Conditioning) company raising capital to acquire small mom-and-pop shops and consolidate for operational efficiency, a sector she knows from her uncle's business, where she worked while she was in high school. These firms are past development, focusing on growth or acquisitions, and lowering risk.

The final $1,000? A passion-driven bet, a startup targeting prostate cancer, was inspired by her father's death. It's high-risk due to FDA hurdles, but she's comfortable with a small stake for a cause so personal. Jane figures out that because of the investment limit for non-accredited investors, she has a little of the $20,000 left over and will keep that to re-invest in the opportunities that progress with their milestones.

Moderate Risk

Jane balances stability and growth here. She keeps $10,000 in her three income producers from Chapter Three, her safety net. She invests $6,000 in three late-stage firms with traction, like companies raising capital to bring *additional products to market, expanding through acquisition, or expanding by modifying their product to serve different industry sectors. The remaining $4,000 is spread across four startups in areas she believes in, like sustainable energy or healthcare tech, with some early wins but higher uncertainty. This mix offers moderate risk with potential upside.*

Risk Tolerant

For big rewards and a large return on investment, Jane shifts gears. She puts just $5,000 into income producers, valuing cash flow but prioritizing growth. The other $15,000 funds eight equity deals at $1,875 each, speculative startups in cutting-edge fields like healthcare, AI, or sustainability. She knows half might fail, but if one hits 100x, like that Wefunder success, she's set.

INSIDE SECRET #28

KEEP IN MIND THAT AS JANE GETS HER INVESTMENT BACK FROM HER INCOME-PRODUCING INVESTMENTS, SHE CAN ROLL THAT OVER INTO HIGHER-RISK INVESTMENTS WHILE ALSO ALLOCATING A PORTION OF HER INCOME IN YEAR 3 FOR NEW INCOME-PRODUCING INVESTMENTS.

Jane's healthcare passion influences her picks, like that IoT-blockchain firm, but her risk tolerance shapes the allocation. You can tailor this, too. Maybe you're drawn to HVAC consolidation (a steady, moderate-risk play) or a foldable kayak startup (riskier, passion-driven). The key is aligning your money with your comfort level and interests, using tools like the entrepreneur question list from our resource portal to evaluate deals and score them on a spreadsheet (referenced in Chapter Three).

Jane's story, from her spark of interest in healthcare to her structured Angel Profitability Blueprint, offers a clear path. She started with personal experiences, like her daughter's baby product struggles and workplace healthcare woes, then methodically hunted for solutions on REG CF and Reg A+ platforms. She built a wish list, researched technologies like IoT and blockchain, and tailored her $20,000 across 10 deals based on her risk tolerance, balancing safe bets with passion projects like prostate cancer research.

This isn't just Jane's story; it can be your blueprint, too. You've got the tools: platforms to explore, questions to ask, and a framework to allocate your funds. Crowdfunding's power lies in its accessibility, amplified by SEC updates like REG CF's $5 million cap and Reg A+'s public listing potential.

Jane turned her $20,000 into a plan that's both strategic and meaningful, and you can, too. Start by listing industries or problems you care about, such as healthcare, sustainability, and local trade. Follow Jane's path and make sure you are disciplined with your approach. Consider finding the training you need to feel confident and competent as you build your portfolio. Research one company, set a news alert, and sketch your risk profile. It doesn't need to be perfect; you just need to begin. The deals are out there. Find the one that speaks to you!

The goal of this book is to spark awareness and belief that you can invest for Purpose, Passion & Profit. Should you choose to take advantage of my digital education platform, The Compassionalist Academy, or find a different training system, take steps to learn to walk before you run.

For The Compassionate Capitalist Movement to have a true impact and an equilibrium between companies seeking capital and available investor capital to be achieved, hundreds of thousands of new investors need to jump into the pool and learn to swim. Although the US Treasury and the SEC found in their 2024 studies that the reason there was a shortage of investors was due to the LACK OF:

Awareness, Education, and Tools. I add a 4th to this…. SUCCESS. As the first three are achieved, #4 will come, and word of mouth will attract others into this exciting and profitable wealth creation strategy.

Ch. Five: Mitigating Risk to Increase Odds of Success

Every investment decision you make carries weight, not just for your wallet but for your confidence as an investor. The process begins with understanding your risk tolerance, return expectations, and the non-negotiable principles that align with your financial goals. Jane discovered that a structured approach, like using a scoring system to evaluate opportunities, helped filter out emotional noise and focus on data-driven criteria. But how do you separate the promising opportunities from the pitfalls? Let's break it down.

Clarifying Risk Tolerance

The process started with Jane clarifying her risk tolerance, return expectations, and non-negotiable criteria. Jane needed to develop her 'investor thesis' to help quickly eliminate deals that didn't fit, so she could focus on the opportunities that would fit.

Jane committed to thorough due diligence, even when a regulation crowdfunding platform's flashy video made a startup's VR headset seem like a "sure thing." Her discipline paid off: she avoided a company that didn't really understand the competitive marketplace, the barriers to the sales cycle, and unrealistic market claims.

The *Company Review Assessment Scoring Worksheet* is a tool included in the Investor Resource Portal that was included for those who purchased my book *"Inside Secrets to Angel Investing"* and is available to the members of The Compassionalist Academy, a crowdfunding and angel investing training, which is a simple yet effective tool to create an objective scoring system to assist in discerning between deal opportunities.

Jane rates startups on factors like market validation, team expertise, and financial realism; if a company scored seven or higher, it aligned with her investor thesis. Below 5, she'd dig deeper or walk away. This system saved her from a blockchain IoT startup claiming "$100M revenue by capturing 1% of a $10B market." Without a clear sales strategy, it was fantasy math.

She also leaned on her network; when evaluating a health tech startup, she consulted her son, an IT expert, who flagged their unrealistic 90-day sales cycle. "B2B software takes at least 6 months but as long as 12–18 months if it requires a board decision," he warned. Jane passed, then later invested when the founder revised their capital ask and updated their timeline to reach cash-flow positive, with a revised sales cycle that included a trial period and creating a multi-channel sales strategy.

The initial $2,000 investment in a childcare app startup succeeded because she vetted their feasibility study and sales pipeline: they'd pre-sold 50 clinics on a telehealth platform, proving traction. Contrast that with the REG CF campaign she rejected: AWG – a water-from-air tech company with no sales team in their budget. "Facebook ads won't sell $20K products to municipalities," she noted.

Jane's rules were clear, and she rejected opportunities that made vague claims like "We'll capture 1% of the market" without a customer acquisition plan. She dismissed teams that relied on "friends-as-experts," such as a CFO with no finance background. She walked away from fuzzy math, like financials forecasting hockey-stick growth without explaining costs. By scoring opportunities and trusting her process, Jane turned hope into strategy. As she says, "If you can't explain your investment value proposition in 10 minutes, you're not ready to get a check from me."

Red Flags

One critical red flag is an **unclear value proposition**: if a startup can't articulate why customers need their product or how it solves a specific problem, it's a sign of trouble.

Jane once evaluated a wellness app that promised to "revolutionize self-care" but couldn't explain how it differed from competitors or justify its pricing, a stark contrast to the childcare app she eventually backed, which clearly addressed a gap in telehealth access for paediatric clinics.

Another common pitfall is a **vague target market**; claims like "everyone aged 18–50" or "any business needing efficiency" are red herrings.

Jane rejected a meal-kit startup targeting "busy professionals" without defining geography, income, or dietary preferences, whereas her successful investments *focused on niches like "urban mothers earning $75k+ seeking eco-friendly baby products," where pain points and purchasing power were clear.*

Equally dangerous are **flawed business models** or sales cycles that ignore reality.

Jane flagged a B2B SaaS startup projecting $10M in year one despite having no sales team, no marketing budget, and a product requiring lengthy enterprise contracts, noting, "If they can't explain how they'll acquire customers or what their cost of sales will be, then they will be figuring out on my dime and that creates great risk."

Then there was the "hockey stick" projections that showed soaring revenue after "capturing 1% of a $10B market," a fantasy Jane dismissed in a blockchain startup, pointing out that even 0.1% would demand a sales army, strong customer service, and support team, and millions in marketing, costs the founders hadn't budgeted.

Many angel groups have companies they excitedly invested in without understanding the importance of a capital strategy. A strong capital strategy will include a small seed stage round to get the product developed and validated, followed by incremental rounds that accomplish the milestones while increasing the value of the company. I estimate that between 25% & 40% of angel group portfolios are companies that plateau, forced to grow organically, and not achieve exit milestones simply because they did not raise sufficient capital to maintain the pace of growth expected.

By the time they realized they needed more capital, they had already lost momentum. They become too big for more angel investment, too small for private equity fund investments, and too slow for growth. Reg A+ is the only option for companies in this predicament if they have a strategic pivot, acquisition, or product launch that can get them back on track… or even fast-track them to an exit.

Jane came to understand that capital mismatches lead many companies to plateau and not reach their full potential. Raising $500k to build a $100M company is delusional, as she saw with a hardware startup that underestimated R&D and manufacturing costs, while raising $10M for a pre-revenue AI firm with no clear use of funds often leads to wasted cash, like CEOs buying lobby furniture instead of closing deals.

Another pitfall is that a red flag for experienced angel investors is an undefined or poorly defined **use of funds**. Founders must know how they will use the capital they are raising. They should have proposals or quotes for development contracts. They need to know what positions they will hire for and what the salary compensation will be. They need to know who they will outsource key business functions to, as well as what that annual cost will be. All of this rolls up into the 'ask' for capital. Of course, there will be a portion used to hedge unexpected costs or delays, but it shouldn't be more than 15% of the total use of funds.

Jane rejected a company allocating 30% of capital to "contingency" without specifics, stating, "If they don't know where the money's going, they'll burn it." Similarly, trusting "friends" as the core team can backfire: a CFO who was the founder's college roommate but lacks financial credentials is a lawsuit waiting to happen.

No operational strategy is equally concerning if the plan for handling customer service, R&D, or scaling is a "we'll figure it out" when we have the money and the customers. That translates into "we don't know, and we want to figure it out with the money you invest". That means they won't be using your investment to make revenue and grow; they will be using it to figure out what they need to do to create revenue in order to grow.

Finally, **overvalued startups signal dange**r, like a $20M valuation for a pre-revenue company with just an idea. This is usually due to the founders' fear of losing control of the company and not wanting to raise capital in multiple stages as they prove out their business model and naturally grow in value.

"Unless they've got Melanie Perkins' (serial entrepreneur and founder of Canva) track record," Jane says, "a huge valuation without tangible evidence, it's inflated." Her mantra, "assume every claim is a hypothesis until proven otherwise," guides her approach, turning pitfalls into guardrails by stress-testing assumptions and demanding specificity, one decision at a time.

Materials to Review (and Why They Matter)

When diving into a business opportunity, the materials you review can make or break your decision. The process starts with the executive summary, a concise 1–2 page snapshot of the business. This is the first impression, and it needs to be sharp. If it's littered with jargon or vague promises like "disrupting the industry," the full plan likely isn't clear either. A strong summary immediately answers three questions: What problem exists? Why now? Why this team? Think of it as the hook that convinces you to read further; if it's fuzzy here, the rest may not recover from the fog of vagueness and unanswered questions.

Next comes the business plan, which serves as the company's roadmap. This isn't just a document; it's the backbone of their strategy, detailing the problem they're solving, their proposed solution, the target market, go-to-market strategy, competition, financials, and execution plan. *If any of these elements feel vague or underdeveloped, it's a red flag.* For instance, a startup claiming to "revolutionize healthcare" without addressing regulatory hurdles or scaling logistics might have ambition but lacks the concrete steps to back it up. The plan must answer not just what they're doing but how they'll get it done.

The pitch deck is where storytelling and strategy collide. A compelling deck avoids flashy design as a crutch and focuses on substance. It should open with a 30-second elevator pitch that's memorable and specific, like "Reducing hospital waste by \$5B annually through smarter inventory systems." From there, it drills into the problem with urgency, using concrete examples instead of generic terms like "inefficient workflows." The solution follows, backed by validation, data, case studies, or demos. For example, a startup might showcase IoT sensors that cut farm water waste by 30%, proving their tech works with a demo, a video, or a third-party validation report. These may be explained in detail in the business plan and just appear as a bullet point on a pitch deck.

The pitch narrative then narrows to the market size and customer targeting. Broad claims like "everyone aged 18–50" are too vague; specificity matters. While the pitch might focus on urban professionals with dietary restrictions earning over $75k, showing a clear, addressable audience, the business plan will explain how that target market was identified. The business model and sales cycle come next, emphasizing realism. If a B2B (Business to Business) SaaS (Software as a Service) company claims a 90-day sales cycle, that's a warning.

Jane used the support team she cultivated to turn to with questions about technology. Her son, for instance, explained to her that enterprise sales cycles typically take 12–18 months, and when she talked to the head of technology at the hospital where she works, he told her they were in the middle of a 6-month trial of a SaaS based patient management subscription service.

Barriers to entry and competition are addressed with equal rigor. The business plan must explain in detail what keeps others from copying their idea: proprietary tech, patents, or strategic partnerships. The pitch will hit the highlights. Competition cannot be ignored; instead, the differentiation is clear, like an AI forecasting tool that is more efficient than spreadsheets. Intellectual property and partnerships are validated, as well. They may be footnoted, or the founder may indicate the full report, the patent filing, and whatever is available upon request.

Jane once passed on a MedTech startup whose "patent-pending" tech lacked engineering proof, highlighting the need for tangible evidence. The management team's expertise is critical. Jane rejected a fintech founder with an unqualified CFO but invested in a SaaS team with Salesforce veterans, trusting their domain knowledge.

Financials are scrutinized for realism. The financial history in their financial statements explains what has happened; their forecast projections explain what to expect in the future if they raise the capital needed to bridge the gap to profitability. The financials are one of the first things I look at after the executive summary because to me, they tell the real story. Then the business plan becomes the narrative explaining the financials with data and strategy. Hockey-stick growth projections raise eyebrows, especially if costs for marketing, salaries, or product development are missing.

When Jane first got started, she tapped her accountant's expertise to help her understand the past performance numbers and the company's jump to huge profit in the upcoming year, and he flagged this imbalance instantly.

The use of funds must be detailed, avoiding vague "contingency" line items. It will be a page in the pitch deck, a section in the business plan, and part of the assumptions documented in the financials. Finally, the ask is specific: "$1M for 10% equity to scale sales," not a nebulous request. The deck closes with a call to action, tying everything back to the startup's mission.

Secondary documents like feasibility studies, competitive analyses, and org charts reveal whether the team has thought through execution. These materials separate prepared founders, with the potential to achieve their vision for their business, from dreamers.

Jane's process, scoring systems, expert consultations, and emotional discipline turn uncertainty into strategy. It's not just about spotting flaws but understanding how gaps could derail success. In the end, diligence transforms luck into informed decisions. The materials you review aren't just paperwork; they're a blueprint for whether an idea can survive the real world. The magic isn't in the idea alone; it's in the execution, and that's only possible when the groundwork is thorough, realistic, and backed by evidence.

INSIDE SECRET: #29

EXPERIENCED ANGEL INVESTORS USE THE EXECUTIVE SUMMARY TO DETERMINE IF THEY WANT TO INVEST ANY TIME IN A MEETING OR REVIEWING THE PITCH. THE PITCH HELPS THEM DETERMINE WHETHER TO SPEND AN HOUR REVIEWING THE BUSINESS PLAN. THE FINANCIALS TELL THE REAL STORY OF PREPAREDNESS. THEN, THE BUSINESS PLAN IS THE VEHICLE TO EXPLAIN THE FINANCIALS, ASK QUESTIONS, AND USE FUNDS. THE PITCH DECK, FOR ME, SIMPLY IS A TOOL TO TELL THE STORY OF THE BUSINESS MODEL, STRATEGY, AND OUTCOME IN PICTURES.

Leverage Experts

When evaluating an investment, the devil is in the details, and professionals like financing consultants, accountants, and lawyers are your allies in spotting them. Jane learned early that even a $250 investment deserves scrutiny. For someone in Jane's financial position, a $250 investment is much like the typical millionaire angel investor's $25,000 investment. Can the financials survive reality? If a startup projects exponential revenue growth but ignores costs like supplier payment delays (e.g., Walmart's infamously slow payouts), an experienced consultant or friend in that industry will flag it. They'll also question assumptions, like a consumer-focused SaaS company claiming "negative churn" (no loss in customers after the initial subscription period) without proof of key performance indicators (KPI) such as customers' average length of contracts and renewals.

For Jane, hiring a pro wasn't a cost; it was insurance against costly oversights. Each time she hired or bartered for expert insight, she came prepared with questions and made sure she understood. After a few deals, she got good at doing the assessment and review herself.

Although they can be pricy when hired directly, lawyers' legal opinions matter just as much. Fortunately, there are now affordable 'member' offerings for legal advice through online portals.

When a crowdfunding deal required signing a SAFE note, Jane didn't wing it; she consulted a securities attorney. The attorney clarified how dilution could erode her stake if the startup issued more shares later. Without that advice, Jane might have overlooked clauses that could halve her ownership in future rounds.

Legal experts also spot ambiguities in contracts, like vague intellectual property terms or compliance gaps. For example, a cannabis startup's failure to address state vs. federal law conflicts could tank its viability, no matter how solid the product is. Patents are valuable, but they need to be applied when the company knows the product works and that the product is market-fit for the solution.

Jane once avoided a VR headset startup that skipped this step, only to burn $50k on a patent for a design that failed basic user tests. They had raised it from their 'friends and family' that was excited about the idea, but they were way ahead of their time, and the underlying technology needed to be advanced before their specific invention could be realized.

INSIDE SECRET: #30

PATENTS CAN BE MISUNDERSTOOD IN TERMS OF THEIR VALUE. A PATENT DOES NOT MEAN THE SOLUTION WORKS; IT JUST INDICATES THAT IT IS UNIQUE. A PATENT IS BEST CONSIDERED AS A BARRIER TO ENTRY, A PROTECTION OF A COMPANY'S MARKET ONCE THE SOLUTION IS DEVELOPED AND IN THE MARKET, GENERATING SALES.

Backup Reports for Validation

Beyond financials and legalities, documents proving viability separate tangible business solutions from vaporware. A feasibility study isn't optional; it's proof that the product can be built and sold if the company does not have commercially available products. Keep in mind that often, a seed-stage company doesn't have a working product. They may just have a design or an idea, and the reason they are raising capital is to design and build it. A startup company might have a prototype, but it needs to go through the process of commercialization, and that is why they are raising that round of capital.

Similarly, a competitive analysis can't claim "no competition." Even disruptors must explain how they'll unseat incumbents. Sometimes this may be in a SWOT analysis (Strengths, Weaknesses, Opportunities, and Threats) that paints a picture of all the companies in an industry as compared to the company entering the market.

There is never a time when there is NO COMPETITION. Even when the company's new product is innovative and novel, the market has been solving that problem in some way with what was available then. For example, when IBM came out with its first computers, there was nothing else like it, but back then, businesses wrote letters and created financial statements with typewriters. Typewriters were the status quo solution at the beginning of the PC era. IBM had to sell against its own products and emphasize that the efficiency gained was greater than the cost of the new equipment.

Jane pressed companies she was considering after looking at their documents and reviewing their FAQ – Frequently Asked Questions. She would submit a question if they didn't explain their competitive advantages well: How would they convince customers to abandon familiar tools? The answer, "We'll be cheaper," wasn't enough since legacy systems often win through inertia.

A marketing strategy that would supplement the business plan would explain beyond a generic strategy, such as "we'll use Facebook ads."

Jane looks for layered plans: How will they build awareness and convert leads? For high-ticket items, like a $10k B2B software, a drip campaign or free trial might work better than generic ads. Then there's the sales pipeline; if a founder boasts $1M in "pending deals" but has no signed contracts or LOIs, it's a bluff. Jane once grilled a startup claiming $500k in commitments, only to find the "deals" were verbal nods from the sales reps working a booth at a trade show, not legally binding agreements.

Every document tells a story. The feasibility study reveals whether the product is technically possible. The competitive analysis shows if the team understands its battlefield. The marketing strategy and sales pipeline prove they can turn plans into revenue. When a startup skips these, they're not just cutting corners; they're flying blind. Jane's mantra? Trust, but verify. A slick pitch might dazzle, but it's the gritty details, vetted by experts and backed by evidence, that turn risky bets into strategic investments. After all, diligence isn't about skepticism; it's about stacking the odds in your favor.

Questions to Ask Founders

When evaluating a startup, asking the right questions isn't just due diligence. It's the difference between backing a visionary team and funding a shaky hypothesis. These questions are designed to uncover whether founders truly understand their business, their market, and the risks they'll face. Let's walk through a few of them, not as a checklist but conceptually to help you consider how they reveal preparedness and clarity.

Start with the core: What specific need does the company address? If a founder can't articulate this sharply, say, "Hospitals lose $5B annually on unused supplies," they're either solving a vague problem or none at all, by not understanding the root cause. Follow up with why customers would switch to their solution. Jane once rejected a meal-kit startup when its founder admitted, "People might prefer us over grocery shopping," but had no data proving they'd abandon Instacart for a pricier alternative.

Dig into the numbers: The cost of goods sold (COGS) isn't just a line item; it's a reality check. Jane's CPA once flagged a skincare brand claiming COGS of $2 per unit, only to discover they'd excluded shipping and returns. Similarly, the pricing strategy must be grounded. A SaaS founder who said, "We'll charge $99/month because competitors do," learned the hard way when customers balked at the lack of tiered features, and he struggled to generate revenue.

Sales and marketing can't be an afterthought.

Jane drills into specifics with the founders she considers investing in: "How will you find customers beyond Google Ads?" A startup claiming "viral growth" but lacking a referral program or partnerships raised red flags. She also *checks if the sales cycle is baked into financials. One founder projected $1M in Q1 revenue but forgot to account for enterprise sales taking many months, even as long as a year, a gap that nearly sank the company.*

Operational grit matters. The skills needed to start a company are different than the skills needed to build a scalable enterprise.

Can their sales process scale? Jane questioned a B2B hardware startup whose founder closed early deals via personal LinkedIn outreach. "Can a sales rep replicate that?" she asked. They hadn't tested it. Customer backlogs are another test: A MedTech company boasted $500k in "pending orders," but when pressed, admitted the "backlog" was a handshake deal with a single clinic. The sales model, direct, indirect, or outsourced, reveals strategic thinking. A DTC (Direct to Consumer) brand claiming to avoid retailers but needing "awareness campaigns" to drive traffic was caught in a contradiction. Jane also probes founders about the time from lead to revenue. A SaaS startup's 90-day claim unraveled when Jane asked, "But what about onboarding and customization?"

Hiring is a window into culture. Do they have someone responsible for identifying the job roles and skills needed, as well as recruiting and hiring? Building a team can be a challenge for a Startup CEO who is also wearing a lot of hats. Founders can't assume that the people they hire will know what to do in that role, or how to succeed. They must have an employee manual. An extension of their business plan is that a department head knows what the goal of their position is and can be part of building it out with the oversight of the Founders.

Jane rejected a founder who said, "We'll hire sales reps off LinkedIn," with no screening process or training plan. Founder and advisor investments matter, too. She once passed on a startup whose "advisor" had invested $500 but demanded a 5% equity stake, a red flag for misaligned incentives. Additionally, prior vs. current funding tells a story. A startup seeking $2M after raising $200k at a $1M valuation had to explain why the new round didn't tank earlier investors' stakes. Jane also asks, "What if funding is delayed?" A founder who shrugged, "We'll figure it out," lost her trust.

Cash flow delays often break startups. Startups need confidence, but it should be borne from knowledge, not just bravado. Cash is the lifeblood. Without funds, the company can't develop, market, hire, or execute on its plan. Bootstrapping will only get a company so far. They raise funds to bridge the gap between "NOW" and where they need to be "PROFITABLE". The amount of funds must be substantiated by their business plan, and therefore, the use of funds must be specific.

"Marketing" isn't enough. Jane wants the investment prospect to provide details in the key areas, as the map to the target KPIs – Key Performance Indicator line items: "$50k for a PR firm, $20k for SEO tools." If funds are for

cash flow gaps, she demands a plan to fix underlying issues. Revenue projections based on "1% of a $10B market" get pushback. Jane wants unit sales tied to actual pipelines, not wishful math.

Founder motivation isn't just fluff; it is the fabric of what they plan to build. Building a company that can scale is hard, very hard. Understanding a founder's 'why' can help you assess how committed they are to work through the tough times; if the goal is 'bigger than themselves,' they will be humble enough to take coaching. A young black female founder wanted to bring healthier popcorn to market based on her grandma's recipes. She had spunk and worked very hard, but her breakthrough didn't come until she realized she needed to release some control, listen to others with more experience, and agree to the terms the investor(s) were proposing. She finally realized it was **better to be a "Rich Founder, than a Poor CEO."**

The VR headset founder who said, "I wanted to make cool tech," lacked the external validation – do others want it and are willing to pay for it? Jane compared that opportunity to another founder who'd lost a friend to hospital errors and built a safety app that was being beta tested at a small hospital and tracked care from the initial engagement with the EMR – Emergency Medical Response team.

When a company outlines plans to scale and raise capital for expansion, its use of automation tools can indicate true scalability. A startup that still manages payroll in Excel instead of a SaaS accounting and payroll system, or relies on Gmail rather than a CRM for sales and engagement campaigns, may struggle to survive as it grows.

Future funding rounds must align with the strategy. A founder claiming, "We'll never need more money," raised skepticism; scaling often requires follow-on capital. Asking probing questions isn't about catching founders off guard; it is about surfacing the assumptions, gaps, and resilience that define a startup's fate. Jane's rule? If answers feel rehearsed, vague, or defensive, the risk isn't worth the reward. But when founders lean into the tough questions with data, humility, and a clear plan, *that's when diligence turns into opportunity.*

When evaluating a startup, you'll quickly learn that tough questions are the sieve separating viable businesses from wishful thinking. Start by pressing on the sales strategy: "How do you plan to acquire customers in a market where competitors spend $10k per lead?" If a SaaS founder boasts about "low-cost social media ads" but admits they've never tested LinkedIn outreach for enterprise clients, that's a glaring gap, especially when their $5k/month price point demands longer sales cycles. Follow up with, "What's your plan if Google Ads double in cost next quarter?" Or what are your KPIs that show that your ad strategy is working for the top of your sales funnel? What is the nurture campaign and sales rep follow-up to qualify a lead and move them through the sales funnel? A startup with no multifaceted sales strategy and lead channels, like partnerships or events, isn't worth the risk.

Next, dig into the founders' experience with blunt questions: "Have you ever scaled a company from $0 to $10M? What went wrong last time?" If a founder admits their prior venture collapsed due to overspending on office space and now champions a remote-first, lean-budget approach, that's a red flag turned into a lesson. But if they claim "nothing went wrong," proceed with caution: they're either inexperienced or unwilling to learn from failure.

Team roles must be crystal clear. Ask, "Who's responsible for closing enterprise deals? Do they have industry experience?" If a health-tech startup's sales lead only has experience selling gym memberships, not six-figure SaaS contracts, you'd question their ability to navigate procurement hurdles. Contrast that with a fintech team where the VP of sales spent a decade at Oracle, mastering complex deals. Startups often don't have a full management team and mid-level or entry-level personnel. That is likely what they will use part of their capital raise for. Even then, they should have a clear idea of the hiring priorities and job descriptions, and key people on the sidelines as advisors waiting for the capital to come in for them to get started full-time and then fill out their team according to the business strategy.

The revenue plan needs to address churn head-on: "What's your customer churn rate? How will you offset it?" A fitness app founder citing "5% monthly churn" but offering no retention strategy, like loyalty discounts or exclusive content, is a liability. Favor teams that turned churn around, like a B2B tool that added quarterly business reviews to upsell features, slashing churn from 20% to 8% in six months.

These questions aren't isolated; they're threads in a larger scheme. By asking these questions, you're testing whether the sales plan aligns with pricing and team expertise and whether the revenue model accounts for churn and market saturation. If a startup claims, "we'll grow 300% annually," tie it back to systems: "How many reps will you hire? What's their quota?" Vague answers unravel the entire narrative. Even small details matter.

Delegating sales to a rookie without oversight risks bottlenecks. Blaming past failures on "bad luck" instead of poor cash flow management reveals a lack of accountability. The mantra here is simple: Every claim must have a system or strategy behind it.

Your approach to evaluating opportunities hinges on a disciplined blend of skepticism and strategy, where curiosity and rigor intersect to cut through the noise of entrepreneurial optimism. By anchoring decisions in structured criteria, market validation, financial realism, and team expertise, you transform uncertainty into actionable insight, turning the abstract "what if" into the concrete "what must be." Tough questions become more than due diligence; they act as a sieve, separating plausible visions from executable plans, while leveraging experts to stress-test assumptions ensures optimism is grounded in evidence, not wishful thinking.

Conclusion

Investing in crowdfunding isn't just about putting money into startups or small businesses; it's about aligning your financial goals with your values, passions, and vision for the future. This journey is deeply personal yet universally accessible, thanks to platforms that democratize investment opportunities once reserved for the wealthy elite.

Whether you're driven by a desire to support innovation, create meaningful change, or build long-term wealth, crowdfunding offers a unique avenue to achieve all three. But as with any investment, success doesn't come from blind enthusiasm; it stems from careful planning, disciplined decision-making, and continuous learning. Let's explore how this process unfolds, using Jane's story as both an example and a blueprint.

Jane's approach to crowdfunding wasn't random; it was methodical. She began by identifying industries she cared about, such as healthcare and sustainability, areas where her personal experiences gave her insight and motivation.

Her father's battle with prostate cancer inspired her to back a high-risk biotech startup working on treatments, a move __rooted in emotion but tempered by realism.__ While the cause was close to her heart, she allocated only a small portion of her portfolio to this venture, recognizing its inherent risks due to regulatory hurdles and scientific uncertainty.

Meanwhile, she balanced these passion-driven bets with safer investments in late-stage companies focused on expansion or acquisitions. These firms offered lower risk because they had proven track records and revenue streams, making them more predictable than early-stage ventures. By blending her interests with a structured strategy, Jane created a diversified portfolio that reflected both her values and her financial goals.

The key to Jane's success lay not only in what she invested in but also in how she invested. Tools like *The Wealth & Liquidity Calculator* helped her evaluate her financial situation before committing funds. Understanding liquidity and how much of her assets could be tied up without jeopardizing short-term needs was critical.

For instance, Jane redirected $20,000 from savings earmarked for a down payment on an income-producing rental property to investing in equity and financing small businesses, knowing she could still meet essential expenses and emergencies. This clarity allowed her to invest confidently, avoiding the stress that often accompanies illiquid investments.

It's a reminder that preparation is as important as execution when building a portfolio. Without a solid foundation, even the best opportunities can lead to unnecessary strain, both mentally and financially.

Once ready to dive into investing in the deals she had identified and been tracking, Jane relied heavily on vetting

processes outlined in resources available in the Compassionalist Academy course materials.

Many of the tools referenced throughout Jane's journey were part of the resource portal included with my first book, *Inside Secrets to Angel Investing- Step-by-Step Strategies to Leverage Private Equity Investment for Passive Wealth Creation.* A digital copy of that book and all the resources are part of *The Compassionalist Academy.*

These tools guided her through evaluating business plans, assessing founders' track records, and scrutinizing financial projections. One particularly effective method was the *Company Review Assessment Scoring Tool,* which forced her to assign objective scores to startups based on criteria like market validation, team expertise, and financial realism.

A score below five meant walking away, no matter how compelling the pitch might have seemed. This system kept emotional impulses in check, turning red flags into clear signals to avoid pitfalls.

For example, one Blockchain IoT (Internet of Things) startup claimed it could capture 1% of a $10 billion market, projecting $100 million in revenue. However, without a coherent sales strategy or evidence of customer demand, Jane recognized "fantasy math" and steered clear when she saw it. She was intrigued by the problem being solved and how Blockchain and IoT tech were being used, so she looked for other companies and found a more viable solution and invested in that instead.

Beyond numbers, Jane paid attention to intangibles like founder motivation and operational scalability. The VR headset company she dismissed early on was led by someone whose primary goal was simply to "make cool tech." In contrast, another entrepreneur who lost a friend to hospital errors built a safety app out of genuine conviction and urgency.

Because Jane had followed the formula of the Angel Profitability Blueprint™, she didn't feel rushed to make her equity investments. By passing on the 'cool tech' that had not been validated, she was able to invest in the hospital safety app. She had flagged that company and watched their progress. When they started their beta testing with a small hospital, she knew they were taking the right steps to get to market, and she wanted to help them with a small investment.

These differences matter. Understanding the company's growth plan helped her understand how automation tools could help a startup scale efficiently; if they were still relying on manually inputted data for payroll, HR, and expense management rather than cloud-based and AI operation integration solutions, growth would likely stall.

Every detail, no matter how small, contributed to Jane's overall assessment. When answers felt rehearsed, vague, or defensive during Q&A sessions, she knew the risk outweighed the reward. Conversely, founders who leaned into tough questions with humility and data-driven solutions earned her trust.

The rise of crowdfunding has transformed investing by lowering barriers to entry while increasing transparency. Regulatory updates like REG CF's $5 million cap increase and Reg A+'s public listing potential have made it easier for everyday investors to participate in private markets.

Jane felt motivated and excited. Even after a long day of work, she was so inspired by the passion of the founders and the companies they were building to solve real problems. The idea of owning a piece of, being a shareholder for so many cool companies that were on their way up, was exhilarating.

Yet, accessibility doesn't mean simplicity. Each type of crowdfunding carries nuances worth understanding. Debt-based models provide predictable income streams through revenue-sharing agreements or fixed-term notes, appealing to those seeking near-term and more reliable returns on the capital invested.

Equity crowdfunding, on the other hand, offers a higher upside but comes with greater risk. Startup and early-stage companies have the most potential but with the greatest risk because so much is yet to be proven and built. Sometimes, every box is checked, but for reasons already explained, they may not raise all the capital they need to scale, increasing the risk and lowering the potential return on investment.

Late-stage companies raising capital for growth or acquisitions present less volatility compared to early-stage startups. They have established that they know how to generate profit, and therefore, the cost of their shares is logically higher than that of a company that is just starting up. There is less risk for them to expand with new products or other strategies with your investment capital, which leads to their returns typically being a lower multiple.

Knowing which model fits your risk tolerance and objectives is crucial. Creating a balanced and diverse portfolio is critical to an angel (and crowdfund) investor's success.

Using The Angel Profitability Blueprint™, one of the tools in the Compassionalist Academy, Jane diversified her first 10 investments by including a few that generated income through revenue share and fixed-term loans. That helped her feel more confident about putting her hard-earned savings into a new kind of investment.

It made Jane feel accomplished when she got that first revenue share investment, but still nervous when it came time to make her next equity investment. She wanted to slip into the 'wait and see mode' before moving forward to complete the initial 10 she had committed herself to. And then she would recall the analysis she had seen that compared investing in crowdfunding companies as a drip investment strategy similar to investing in her 401k at work. She had been steadily making those investments every month- just autopay out of her check, she never missed it. She had taken comfort that it was pretty secure until the stock market crash in 2009 and again in 2025 that seemed to do a disappearing magic trick on the value of investment. Jane had heard Karen's podcast talking about

Jason Calacanis' conversation with a pioneer in the crowdfunding industry.

Several years ago, after writing my first book, I was following Jason because he had released his book about angel investing at the same time and we had connected about our books. When I heard Jason share his perspective on the revolutionary way crowdfunding was going to change the capital markets, a paradigm even shifted for me. This summarizes my recollection of what Jason said:

I would tell my 20-something self not to start that first company but go get experience inside a corporation with a good paying job, and instead of investing in the company 401k (because no corporate match for 5 years) I would invest $500 a month into a Reg CF company. I'd invest in what I liked, then watch and learn how they progressed. And at the end of the 5 years, I would have a lot more money than I would in my 401k and tremendous knowledge about business models and triggers for success and failure, even if the outcomes were like in the 'standard' VC portfolio of 10 companies – and I might just then use that to that first company.

Let's take a look at that math and see what Jason was talking about and what gave comfort to Jane to continue on her Crowdfund Investing Journey.

The math is eye-opening.

Imagine this scenario:

$500 invested each month for 5 years = 60 companies and $30,000 total investment.

The VC portfolio average says you will have a mix of losses, moderate gains, and a few big winners that will make up for all the rest. Therefore 60 investments work out to 6 hypothetical portfolios.

For every 10 startups:

1 "big winner" returning 10x on the investment > 10 x $500 = $5000

2 medium wins return at 5x ($5,000 total)

2 small wins at 2x ($2,000)

2 breakeven ($1,000)

3 failures ($0)

→ $13,000 back per $5,000 invested.

Scale that across all six portfolios-- $30,000 becomes $78,000—a $48,000 net gain even with 18 total failures. That's the VC model's power: diversification plus a few runaway successes.

Now contrast that with a typical 401(k) or market index fund. Historically, the average annual rate of return is ~9% before commissions and fees and not adjusted for inflation. Investing the same $6,000/year for 5 years Would generate about $35,900. Solid growth—but far from the $78,000 potential of a diversified REG CF portfolio

Historical Context:

- Over the past **20–30 years**, the **S&P 500** has averaged **~9–10% annually**, *before fees and inflation.*

- After adjusting for inflation (real return), it's closer to **6–7%**.

So, if someone simply invests **$6,000/year** into a **low-fee S&P 500 index fund** and earns a **9% annual return**, they'll still end up with:

💰 **$35,908 after 5 years**, just like in the 401(k) scenario (since the math is based on contributions and compounding at the same rate).

An important point to make is this assumption does not account for fees that financial management firms charge for their management of the retirement fund.

Strategy	Annual Return	5-Year Outcome (on $6K/year)
401(k) – No Match	~9%	~$35,900
Index Fund (S&P 500)	~9%	~$35,900
Crowdfund Portfolio (VC model)	Variable, but the example yields ~36% IRR equivalent	~$78,000 (modeled)

This isn't magic; it's a strategy. By embracing calculated risk and backing innovators (not just indexes), Jane positioned herself for asymmetric returns. Her blueprint? Diversify, vet ruthlessly, and let winners offset losses.

Which brings us back to Jane; she didn't just chase returns; she hunted vision. She stayed on course because she was committed to building the wealth she wanted for her future and to leave for the next generation of her family. She especially valued businesses with clear growth potential, like that childcare app that expanded into senior care she put a little money in to see how they would progress. No "one-trick ponies" for her. With the commitment of time and money, came experience that fortified Jane's patience to find the right fit for her. Patience and discipline in her specific intent were virtues she learned to not underestimate, like balancing early-stage tech (high upside!) with late-stage companies raising capital to launch new products.

For Jane, the process became deeply fulfilling. She wasn't merely allocating capital; she was contributing to missions she believed in. Supporting sustainable energy projects or healthcare innovations gave her a sense of purpose beyond financial gain.

While some investments yielded modest returns within months, others held the promise of substantial payouts years down the line. This balance between near-term profits and long-term growth underscores the importance of patience.

Building a portfolio isn't a sprint; it's a marathon that requires discipline and adaptability.

Jane reassessed her investments annually, adjusting allocations as her circumstances changed. Her son's graduating from college freed up additional funds, allowing her to continue to expand her portfolio thoughtfully beyond the initial $20,000 she had allocated.

Crowdfunding's power lies in its ability to connect people with ideas that resonate personally. Imagine backing a foldable kayak startup if you love outdoor adventures or investing in HVAC consolidation, with a little nostalgic emotion mixed in, if you value steady, moderate risk plays.

These choices reflect who you are and what you care about. Tools like the *Entrepreneur Questions Worksheet* and scoring spreadsheets like the *Company Review Assessment Scoring Worksheet* help turn passions into actionable strategies. They ensure that every dollar invested serves a dual purpose: advancing your financial future while supporting causes you believe in.

Additionally, going through diligence transforms curiosity into confidence. Every document reviewed, every founder questioned, and every red flag identified adds layers of assurance. Feasibility studies reveal whether a product is technically viable. Competitive analyses show whether a team understands its market landscape.

Marketing strategies and sales pipelines prove they can convert plans into revenue. Skipping these steps means you're flying blind. Jane's mantra: *"Trust, but verify;"* encapsulates this mindset perfectly. A slick pitch might dazzle momentarily, but it's the gritty details, vetted thoroughly, that turn risky bets into strategic investments.

As we reflect on Jane's journey, it's clear that crowdfunding isn't just about money but also about participation. You're not a passive investor in a faceless corporation; you are part of a larger mission driving progress in ways that benefit everyone.

There's profound fulfillment in knowing your dollars are working toward something positive, something capable of changing lives and solving problems. **But getting started requires action**. You can begin by listing industries or issues you care about. Sign up with a crowdfunding platform and start to see what is out there. Watch some videos of ideas that seem interesting and set news alerts. Sketch your risk profile and begin to research one or two of the companies.

What else is out there?

It doesn't need to be perfect; you just need to begin. Platforms abound with opportunities waiting to be discovered, each offering the chance to make a difference.

Start educating yourself. You can get free education through my weekly podcast: The Compassionate Capitalist Show. The recordings are available as video and audio on Spotify. Videos of prior episodes are on YouTube @angelinvesting. Audio of the recent shows is available on every major platform where you listen to podcasts. All of the links are available in the call to action.

And when you are ready, consider signing up for **the Intro to Angel and Crowdfund Investing**, which is a course in **The Compassionalist Academy.**

www.Compassionalist.Academy

Discount code in the Call-to-Action Section

Ultimately, the goal isn't perfection, but progress. Mistakes will happen, but they become valuable lessons when approached with humility and a willingness to learn.

Crowdfunding democratizes access to investment opportunities, giving everyday people the tools to shape the future. With diligence, patience, and a commitment to continuous improvement, anyone can navigate this space successfully.

Perhaps one day, you'll look back and realize your investments didn't just grow your portfolio; they helped bring new ideas to life, solved real-world problems, and left a lasting impact.

Isn't that what true wealth is all about?

Isn't that a great way to leave a legacy; to leave your thumbprint on the world?

Acknowledgments

This book would not have been possible without the support of my husband, Jim, on my long and winding road to achieve my goal of being a catalyst for change. I appreciate the time invested and insights offered by him and my friend, Nora Pullen, to help me fine-tune this book.

Furthermore, I would be remiss if I didn't acknowledge colleagues and friends who have been around me on this journey. They opened doors, made connections, and helped me to have a seat at the table to learn about this dynamic and evolving industry of crowdfunding, so that I could be a champion of change in how we think about wealth creation.

In no particular order, I'd like to thank:

Devin Thorpe	Dara Albright
Ruth Hedges	Terrence Gallman
Rep. Dar'shun Kendricks	Jonny Price
Sherwood (Woodie) Neiss	Chris Lustrino
Christopher Miller	Karl Dakin
Topiltzin Gomez	David V Duccini
Gene Massey	Dina Ellis Rochkind
Kathleen Minogue	Jenny Kassan
John Moye	Steve Justice
Erik Nelson	David Weild IV

Call to Action

Join the Compassionate Capitalist Movement and Continue Your Journey

Ready to Start Investing with Purpose, Passion, and Profit? Jane's journey doesn't end here—and neither should yours.

To take the next step and become a confident, competent crowdfund investor, join me inside The Compassionalist Academy —a digital learning platform designed to give you the tools, strategies, and confidence to build wealth by investing in startups and small businesses that align with your values.

You can start at the entry level and move through advanced angel investor strategies. As you complete the modules, you will receive a Certificate of Completion. Included with your subscription is the digital version of Karen's first book that launched the movement: *Inside Secrets to Angel Investing*, and The Resource Portal with all the worksheets referenced here and more.

Get started today at: www.Compassionalist.Academy

With your purchase of this book, get 10% off your total first course subscription or purchase with code: JANE10

Because wealth building shouldn't be a privilege—it should be your right.

To find links to Karen's podcast The Compassionate Capitalist Show, her social media and even schedule a call, visit her linktree: http://bit.ly/linkCCS